Life's Greatest Questions

A thought for each day of the year.

Philip M. Hudson

Copyright 2021 by Philip M. Hudson.

Published 2020.

Printed in the United States of America.

All rights reserved.

No portion of this book may be reproduced, stored in a retrieval system, or transmitted in any form or by any means - electronic, mechanical, photocopy, recording, scanning, or other - except for brief quotations in critical reviews or articles, without the prior written permission of the author.

ISBN 978-1-950647-36-1

Illustrations - Google Images.

This book may be ordered from online bookstores.

Publishing Services by BookCrafters
Parker, Colorado.
www.bookcrafters.net

Table of Contents

Thoughts For Each Day Of The Year..1 - 372
Where Did We Come From?..1
Why Are We Here?..125
Where Are We Going?...249

About The Author..373
By The Author...375
What More Can I Say?..379

Without the softening influence that is one of the blessings that comes to us from the Spirit, we tend to suffer both hard hearts and stiff-necks. We are overtly and covertly rebellious. We lack the malleability and the pliability that were cultivated during spiritual therapy before we came to earth.

Acknowledgements

In this volume, I have attributed quotations to original authors whenever possible, as well as when I have editorialized their ideas. In many cases, however, my language will naturally reflect the teachings of leaders and members of The Church of Jesus Christ of Latter-day Saints.

The list of those who have contributed to this book is endless. As I have organized my own thoughts, I have realized how heavily I have borrowed from the towering examples of those who, over the years, have been my mystical mentors, my sensible chaperones, my spiritual guides, my surrogate saviors, my compassionate critics, and everything in between.

They are my avatars, manifestations of deity in bodily forms, my na'vi, the visionaries, who communicate with God on a level to which I can only aspire, and my tsaddik, whom I esteem as intuitive interpreters of biblical law and scripture. They are my divine teachers incarnate. They have offered listening ears, extended open arms. lifted my spirits, shown me the way, stretched my mind, reinforced my faith, strengthened my testimony, helped me to discover my wings, given immaterial support, provided of their means, emboldened me with words of encouragement, cheered me on with wise counsel, taught me humility, been there to steady me, soothed my troubled soul, stepped in to nurture me, led me to fountains of living water, wet my parched lips with inspired counsel, and bound up my wounds.

When I think of the influence of a multitude of angels thinly disguised as my family, friends, and peers, I remember the words of Sir Isaac Newton, who, when pressed to reveal the great secret behind his accomplishments, simply replied: "I stood on the shoulders of giants." Of course, at the end of the day, I alone am responsible for the content of this volume. But I hope my interpretations of principles and doctrine will cultivate your interest to dig deeper into the themes woven into this tapestry, by turning to the scriptures and seeking inspiration from the Spirit. My only goal is to help you to expand your insights into the telestial mile markers, the terrestrial truths, and the celestial guidelines that accompany each of us during our quest for enlightenment as we ponder life's greatest questions.

Faith is dead, without the accompanying work of repentance that is made possible by the Atonement, Christ's sacrifice from before the foundation of the world. Even great faith has not the power to save us from the unalterable demands of Justice. So that Mercy might prevail, God's Plan provided One Who was willing and able to be a Mediator.

We do not
live in a Garden
setting as did our first
parents. Instead, opposition
exists as the foundation of a
matrix of mayhem, within which
the fiery darts of the adversary
will surely continue to trace an
incendiary trail of disorder
across an earthly sky.

Preface

I love to learn by reading the scriptures, and I often think of St. Hilary, who wrote in the third century: "Scripture consists not in what we read, but in what we understand." In each of the musings within this volume, I have consistently tried to find a scriptural foundation and a spiritual confirmation as I put my pen to paper.

I am continually reminded of Nephi's counsel to press forward with complete dedication and steadfastness, or confidence with a firm determination in Christ, having a perfect brightness of hope, or perfect faith, and charity, or a love of God and of all men. If we do this, feasting upon the word of Christ, or receiving strength and nourishment as we ponder the doctrines of the kingdom, and particularly those that relate to life's greatest questions, and as we then endure to the end in righteousness, we shall have eternal life, which is the greatest of God's gifts. (See 2 Nephi 31:20).

It is with love, then, that I extend to you the invitation to enjoy this omnibus of random thoughts. Embrace it at face value, and use its observations as a springboard to your own personal plateaus of discovery, as you are taught by the Spirit to move in the direction of your dreams.

We
who have
the faith to
be born again
are set free by the
Atonement of Christ
to reach our potential.
We are as the acorns of
mighty oaks, vitalized by
faith and basking in the
nurturing influence of
God to grow to the
full stature of
our spirits.

Introduction

If they are fortunate, novice quilters quickly learn a bit of wisdom from the Amish, who make some of the finest quilts in the world. On purpose, the Amish build mistakes into their projects, because they believe that any attempt on their part to design and produce a flawless creation would be a mockery of God, Who alone is perfect. The humility of the Amish makes me think of my own weak attempts to put the thoughts expressed in this omnibus to paper. In His infinite wisdom, God knows very well that I do not need to consciously plan on lacing my efforts with errors. That will come quite naturally, without the need for me to intentionally contribute to my short-comings.

Perhaps this serendipitous collection of musings will do little more than help to define quirks in my personality. Each of us is different, and many things, including our family and friends, the circumstances in which we find ourselves, the quality of our education, and our own personalities, inspire and mold our oral and written expressions. I would like to think that, in this text, all of these influences have been encouraging, affirmative, and constructive.

The reflections within this tome leave the door ajar for the reader, to allow shafts of the light of understanding to creep in. If, as I have expressed my thoughts, I mis-stated myself a few times, or flat-out got it wrong, I ask the patient indulgence and gentle correction of the reader.

Too often, I realize that my communications can be "carefully disguised with hypocrisy and glittering words," as Einstein put it. Although I do fancy myself a wordsmith, I have tried to avoid pedestrian expressions, idle language, and lazy scholarship. I do not pretend to be an authority on Life's Greatest Questions, inasmuch as I believe that we are all works in progress, but if you find the factual tone of a particular musing disengaging, the truth is that I typically experienced a deep personal involvement in my interpretation of the principles that illuminated its meaning.

In any event, when you open this volume, I hope you ponder these minute musings with as much enjoyment as I have experienced while creating them.

Where did we come from?

It is only the Atonement, that was envisioned by God from before the foundation of the world, that has the power to unshackle us from the unpleasant demands that, in the absence of Mercy, would have otherwise been imposed upon all of us by Justice. While darkness is the conjoined twin of misery, the obedience of faith frees us to embrace the truth, to make intelligent choices, to perform purposefully, to carry on convincingly, and to progress persistently. In short, we may rise above all of the cares of the world through the sacrifice for our sins of omission and commission, and all of our shortcomings that lie in between.

The Spirit loves to touch our heart strings to remind us that we were once fluent in the heavenly language that was spoken in our pre-mortal home. Even now, His voice is rhythmical and melodious, soothing to our ears and calming to our souls. When we hear the Spirit whisper: "You're a stranger here", we are comforted with the reassurance that all of us have somehow "wandered from a more exalted sphere." (Eliza R. Snow). The Holy Ghost will prompt us to examine what it means to be anxiously engaged. He will inspire us as we plumb the depths of our commitment to Jesus Christ, sensitize us to the nobility of His work, expand upon our vision of immortality, personalize the Atonement, and help us to remain consciously aware of our close proximity to heaven, that we left only recently, because it was our turn to come to earth.

The Plan of Salvation is so magnificent that when it was presented to those who had collectively assembled in the Council, "the morning stars sang together, and all the sons of God shouted for joy." (Job 38:7-8). The principle of equality taught by the Gospel makes it inconceivable that a Plan of such transcendent perfection would have been designed to redeem in the Celestial Kingdom only a tiny percentage of the children of God. To believe such begs credulity and seems to dismiss as a thing of naught His mission statement, which is to bring to pass not only our immortality, but also our eternal life. After all, is not the Atonement both infinite and eternal in its scope?

The Gospel
teaches us that our
Heavenly Father is the
Grand Architect of a divine
design that establishes our familial
roots and confirms His fatherhood, that
we might enjoy a witness that it is in Him
alone that "we live, and move, and have our
being; as certain also of (our) own poets have
said. For we are also his offspring." (Acts 17:28).
When we seek to understand ourselves from an
eternal perspective, we raise our sights to the
possibility of an expanded view of life, and
we are up and moving forward on the
pathway to personal re-discovery
and religious re-cognition.

The cataracts of confusion that are the consequence of our concessions to sin, and that remain unanswered thru repentance, create swirling mists of darkness that will cloud our vision. Our narrow perspective will force us into making comfortless compromises that will leave the landscapes of our lives as empty shells. If we do not take advantage of the therapy offered by the Lord Jesus Christ, the prognosis must remain poor. He is a heavenly optometrist for weary eyes that have lost the ability to see clearly and that can no longer make the distinction between good and evil and between light and darkness, and even between pleasure and pain. He is the only One Who can restore our vision to the 20:20 acuity we enjoyed before we came to earth.

When we sell
our souls to the Devil
for a mess of pottage, we are
dragged down to a hell on earth
that is of our own construction. Our
bad habits are the result of repetitively
impulsive behaviors that, in rising tides of
wickedness, continually erode away at the
foundations of faith. We are fettered by the
chains of our compulsions, and only too late
realize that our unlimited freedom has led
to tyranny. No-one but our Savior has the
power to lead us from the precipice of
destruction, back along the path of
safety to the security of the perfect
law of liberty that we enjoyed in
our heavenly home before
our births.

The Spirit extends to us the opportunity to experience the ambiance of our divine domicile. It is there that we will return to the warm embrace of our Heavenly Father, His Son Jesus Christ, and the Holy Ghost Who will carry us to the edge of eternity itself. At the portals of heaven, forever will be revealed before us, as in a mind-bending panorama. In the meantime, we are reassured that it was an integral element of The Plan of God, that was confirmed by the Council from before the foundation of the world, that children who died before the age of accountability would be saved in the Celestial Kingdom by the power of the Atonement. "If not so, God is a partial God, and also a changeable God, and a respecter of persons," as we struggle with the reality of so many innocent children who have died without baptism! (Moroni 8:12).

The adversary, who is ever the consummate con man and the master deceiver who was a liar from the beginning, even now continues his efforts to subvert the execution of The Plan of Salvation and the education of all of God's children, by the substitution of his counterfeit proposal. That despairing and unworkable alternative would have required neither repentance nor Atonement by our Savior. Fortunately, at the Council in Heaven, when the merits of both plans were discussed, we were able to see through his deception. Today, the actions of those who have retained their eternal perspective reflect their continuing determination to be counted among the disciples of Christ.

Before the
world's creation,
our Father knew that
we would find our strength
only thru the infinite power of
the sacrifice of His firstborn Son.
As we continue to seek the Lord while
He may be found, a Constant Companion
will teach us how we may become better
engaged in fashioning defensive weapons
in our armory of thought. It is with these
tools that the Spirit will guide us and
direct us. He will show us just what
we need to do in order to build
our heavenly fortifications of
love, joy, strength, service,
compassion, testimony,
conversion, and
peace, thru the
Atonement.

In the endowment in
the temple we witness not
only the best of power, but also
the worst of violence, and we see
that they are mutually exclusive; where
one is present the other must be absent. We
learn about the satanic inclination to abuse
authority, and we discover that those who have
it may be least prepared for positions of trust
and responsibility. As the drama unfolds, we
discern a basic mathematical theorem:
that the principles of God's perfect
Plan operate more by addition
than by subtraction.

If Heavenly Father had not provided a Redeemer to atone for their sins, if Adam and Eve were to have partaken of the fruit of the Tree of Life, which is eternal life, it would have been impossible for them to enjoy celestial glory. In their fallen state without repentance and forgiveness of their sins, there would have been no avenue of escape. They would have been incapable of obedience to celestial law, and would have lived forever in their sins. Therefore, the Great Plan of Redemption would have been frustrated, and our common enemy Lucifer would have not only carried the day, but he would also have won the war in heaven.

How many times have we read about, or even witnessed, cultural collapse because a faithless society has decayed from within? In every case, iniquity follows those who yield themselves "unto the power of Satan." (3 Nephi 7:5). The world does not seem to be able to understand that Lucifer was a first-grade dropout whose influence was the companion of anarchy. As his disciples do to this day, at the Council he dismissed the power of the Atonement, and denied the righteous application of free will to help us work out our salvation before God, angels, and witnesses.

The Spirit
teaches us about
the autobiographical thread
within each of us that leads all
the way back to heaven. When, in the
pre-mortal world, we were handed the
script of life's Three Act Play, we realized
that it had the potential to harvest a Tony
Award; that it could order our chaotic world,
bless us with clarity rather than confusion, and
teach us how to achieve fluency in the language
of the Spirit. The Plan would educate those who
had been functionally illiterate in terms of their
Gospel scholarship, so that all might be equally
mesmerized by its recuperative power. The Holy
Ghost helps us to remember that we have been
placed on the earth precisely because it is
a machine for the making of gods.

All of us
are repeatedly
faced with occasions
when withdrawals must be
made from our spiritual bank
accounts. When we respond to the
Spirit, Who drives us to our knees to
help us to recognize the awesome power
of the Atonement, we put the principle of
repentance to its test, as we remember the
promises we made so long ago. But we do
not write checks that can't be cashed. We
realize that only after regular deposits
have been made over a period of time,
can we rely upon the cornucopia of
comfort created by the cushion of
confidence that is a currency
flowing from conduct that
is consistent with the
core curriculum of
contrition.

It is the Holy Ghost Who reintroduces us to the power of the Atonement, that can save us from our natural state of carnality, sensuality, and devilish inclinations. It activates the Law of Mercy, which mitigates for those who conform to its requirements the effects of the first Law, that demands justice. It lifts us to a state of holiness, spirituality, angelic innocence, and happiness. It prepares us to feel comfortable in our heavenly home, where we will find ourselves once again in the presence of angels who are softly singing celestial lullabies that express only love. The Holy Ghost will be there as well, to welcome us back home.

Standing in
opposition to the
light of the Spirit is
a darkness that has the
potential to cover the earth,
and gross darkness the people.
Without the influence of the Holy
Ghost to intervene in our behalf by
introducing us to the Atonement, we
would be held captive by the source of
that gloom, to rise no more. The Devil,
who was a liar from the beginning, even
now continues his efforts to foil The Plan
by the substitution of his own counterfeit,
unworkable alternative that would not
require repentance or the Atonement.
Fortunately, in the setting of the
Council in heaven, we could see
through his deception. Because
of the guidance of the Spirit,
sent by our Heavenly Father
to accompany us on our
journey thru mortality,
our vision remains
unclouded.

Armed with the power that stems from the Holy Ghost, our innermost longings to apprehend visions of the eternal world are epitomized by our triumphant realization of dreams fulfilled. In the expression of our testimonies, our emotions are painted by the words and symbols that depict our progression toward the distant mileposts that mark the way we must all follow as we journey on toward heaven. As we reiterate the expressions of our witness that Jesus is our Savior, it is with faith that we hear the familiar refrains of a celestial symphony that has been scored for every imaginable instrument. In the repertoire of the Holy Ghost, we re-discover the musical melodies that appealed to us in our primeval childhood.

To
the great
relief of grieving
parents, the Atonement
affirms the innocence of
children. It was an integral
element of The Plan that was
ordained in the Council in heaven
before the creation, that little ones
who would pass away before they had
reached the age of accountability would
be saved in eternal glory by the power
of our Savior and our Redeemer. His
influence extends to every corner
of the earth, from the beginning
of the world to the very end
of time. Truly, did He say:
"Suffer the little children
to come unto me."
(Mark 10:4).

If we ignore the celestial laws that are the only homing beacons that are powerful enough to penetrate the swirling mists of darkness that characterize the telestial world to which we have been assigned by Heavenly Father, we have tacitly chosen an alternative course leading to our destruction, as we run aground on rocky coastlines of personal misfortune that are bereft of the influence of the Holy Ghost. On the other hand, the Spirit can become a celestial bridge to transport us past the deviations of life, to the steadiness of the kingdom that rests above the world's instability and turmoil.

Angels will attend us as we repent: "For I will go before your face," promised the Lord. "I will be on your right hand, and on your left, and my Spirit shall be in your hearts, and mine angels round about you, to bear you up." (D&C 84:88). With such a promise from God, how could we think to decline this offer, return to our wicked ways, and determine to go it alone? Such would be a defiant contravention of the reassurance we had been given back in our home in heaven, that He would never leave us.

During the process of our conversion, we slowly become aware of the divine design that has been mapped out for all of us. "Our lives are fairy tales waiting to be written by the finger of God." (H.C. Anderson). Because the Spirit is mindful of The Plan, He will bless us with the regularly recurring reassurance of religious recalibration that autocorrects with fortuitous frequency and with celestial precision. He is always waiting in the wings to assist us if we stumble, or if we have forgotten the lines that we had earlier memorized for the second of the Three Acts of the Plan of God.

It is by our faith to see all the way to heaven that the power of the Spirit is released. It can penetrate the barriers that isolate us from the sum and the substance of our existence that more accurately define our characters as beings of light who have come down from a heavenly home, trailing clouds of glory. As we ascend a ladder of faith, rung by rung, to be firmly and securely reintroduced to the potency of the Spirit, we will see lightnings, and mountains smoking, and we will perceive the voices of trumpets and thunderings that speak to our souls in a language that is inarticulate, but is yet irrefutable.

It is
our honesty
with ourselves and
with the Holy Ghost
that tests the mettle of
our convictions. Through
our repentance, we put our
money where our mouth is. We
have no proof until we act on
the basis of trust. Then, comes
the confirmation of the reality
as feelings of self-confidence
grow and purposeful actions
replace tentative overtures.
In sum, we let go and we
let our Father do what He
promised us before we
left our heavenly
home.

As
our circle
of knowledge
expands under
the influence of
the Spirit within us,
so do the borders of
darkness. The more we
know, the more we need
to learn. It should do no
violence to our faith if we
realize that, with a greater
understanding of truth, we
will surely have additional
questions that we wish to
ponder, even those that
relate to the mystery
of our lives before
our births.

In the world, there is a subtle and yet pervasive negative energy whose most effective countermeasures are the promptings that come to us from the Holy Ghost. His antidote stipulates that when, in any magnitude, we embrace the opposites that lie before us, we immediately implement the safety protocols required by repentance. These serve to reorient our focus so that it remains firmly fixed upon the Atonement, so that we may more clearly see all the way to back to heaven, to our spiritual roots.

Those of weak
will, who turn away
from the gentle promptings
of the Holy Ghost, gradually lose
their focus, just as their eyesight may be
lost over time. First, they squint, and then
they hold the page a little closer or a little
further away, compensating for their inability
to see clearly. Whether it is the printed page or
their integrity that they cannot read, without
the Spirit, there will be character crippling
compromises, as well as a demoralizing
crash of conscience. These are feelings
that were flying beneath the radar
when we were preparing to leave
our home in heaven. Thanks be
to the Spirit, Who always
has our back.

The ordinance of the
endowment in the House
of the Lord provides a glimpse
of what it must have been like in
our pre-mortal existence, and then
it explains the purpose of life on earth.
Lastly, it opens our hearts and our minds
to soul-expanding eternal opportunities.
When we conform to its overall strategy
for success, we become better friends,
neighbors, and witnesses of Christ. If
we have done the math and crunch
the numbers, we will also be better
prepared to deal with the elusive
equations that define true
happiness.

When designing
The Plan, God knew
that, with only nine months
to put the final touches on our
preparations, we would transition
from the eternal world where we had
enjoyed the warmth of hearth and home
in heaven, to the bleak atmosphere of the
lone and dreary world here on earth. When
we did so, we knew that there would be an
immediate disconnect that would be both
brutal and unrelenting in its intensity.
It is that disengagement that makes
it imperative that we find our way
to the sanctuaries of the Spirit
that our Heavenly Father
has provided for us.

When
we faithfully
persist in the process
of repentance, the Spirit
will teach us how to become
engaged in fashioning defensive
weapons in the armory of thought.
With these tools, the Holy Ghost will
show us how to reconfigure the arsenal
of heavenly munitions with which we
are already familiar. He will bring
to our remembrance the firearms
safety course that we completed
in a premortal setting, that
focused on faith, hope,
and charity, as well
as peace, strength,
and joy.

Before we left home,
our Heavenly Father explained
to us that, after our arrival on the
earth, we would become acquainted with
pain as well as with pleasure, with evil as
well as with good, with darkness as well as
with light, with error as well as with truth,
and with punishment for the violation of
His celestial statutes, as well as with the
blessings that would follow obedience.
We were reassured, however, that the
Holy Ghost would always be there
if things were to get rough for
us during these character
building experiences.

The Great Plan of
Mercy, that was conceived by
our Father and introduced to the
Council, envisions a Utopian society,
but it is at the same time pragmatic.
It anticipated our weaknesses and
provided us with the Atonement as
a practical solution for those of
us (meaning all of us) whose
agency would lead them
away from the Rod of
Iron and the fruit
of the Tree of
Life.

The genius of
the Atonement that
was conceived in heaven
from before the foundation
of the world, is that it has the
reach to nurture our relationship
with our Heavenly Father, the Savior,
and the Spirit. It frees us to become
the fashioners of our fortunes, even
as we learn to rely upon resources
that are greater than ourselves
for each breath that we take,
whether it be celestial air,
or telestial greenhouse
gas emissions.

Our family ties can be traced all the way back to Adam and Eve, who were the offspring of our Heavenly Father. Every member of our family is the physical and spiritual reminder of our Heavenly Father, and so, we become legitimate heirs, through our faithfulness, of all that He is. Our families provide the context we need, so that we may work to become more like Him. Families provide the tapestry upon which is stitched the words to the Primary song: "I am a child of God." (Naomi Randall).

Through the workings of the Holy Ghost and by the power of our faith, we can see all the way into eternity, with the capacity to be carried beyond the perceptible and palpable confines of this world. We return in our minds' eye to our former abode in heaven, where boundaries are blurred and the barricade of borders evaporates in a flood of light. The Plan of God was carefully crafted to create the conditions wherein we would be strengthened by the Holy Ghost to do our best within the cradle and crucible of our experience in mortality.

The Holy Ghost
blesses us with the
knowledge that mortality
is only a very small sliver of
a much larger view of life, and
that our perspective is faulty only
when we believe it to be unique. This
knowledge of our divine heritage acts as
a catalyst, inspiring us to be our very best.
At the same time, it is the fragmentation of
balance and order that creates the friction
that fuels the fire of the Spirit to warm the
world. One could even say that it is the
opposition that we encounter that
makes life on the strait and
narrow path possible.

If we allow ourselves to sink into the quicksand of carnality and lose the wide eyed innocence of youth, and with it our purity as well as our holiness, we will surely forfeit the happiness that can only accompany untroubled souls. On the other hand, if the Spirit molds us in mortality it will establish us in eternity. We will one day find ourselves encircled by the same heavenly smiles and enjoy the beat of the same music of those celestial symphonies with which we were undoubtedly familiar in our pre-mortal home.

Our divine
right to exercise free
will within an atmosphere of
opposition has been intertwined
with creation itself. In our second
estate, the Gospel of Jesus Christ prepares
us to move onward without encumbering us
with wobbly constraints of uncertainty that are
the telestial manifestations of devilishly designed
deviations and distractions. It is God's Plan of
Salvation that makes our lives eternal and our
loves immortal. It is only within its context
that the joy of birth, as well as the stark
reality and inevitability of death,
are transformed into horizons
that are nothing, save the
limits of our sight.

It is in the temple endowment
that our Heavenly Father has provided
a way for us to return to the secret garden
of our childhood, that we might fully mature.
As Wordsworth wrote: "Heaven lies about us in our
infancy. Shades of the prison house begin to close
upon the growing boy, but he beholds the light and
whence it flows. He sees it in his joy. The youth,
who daily farther from the east must travel,
still is nature's priest, and by the vision
splendid, is on his way attended. At
length the man perceives it die
away, and fade into the light
of common day."

Our endowment of spiritual
and priesthood power in the House
of The Lord helps us to imagine what
it will be like when we return home from
our mortal mission assignments. It is a dress
rehearsal that was designed to be repetitively
repeated prior to the opening of the final act
of God's Three Act Play. It is difficult for
some to grasp, because it was conceived
in heaven. It is not of this world, and
so, if we intellectually memorize its
lines or try to wrap our finite
minds around it, we will fail
miserably, for it must be
spiritually discerned,
or not at all.

When the scroll
is unfurled that reveals
the ordinances and covenants of
the Gospel, there will be markers that
define the bounds and conditions of the
unknown possibilities of existence. Before
we came to earth, our Father explained
that we would be required to enroll in
the graduate school of hard knocks,
and that we would have to pre-pay
the required tuition, in order to
obtain the credits that were to
be earned by our obedience
to the promptings of the
Holy Ghost.

The guidance that we receive
from the Holy Ghost should be
centered on the revelations the Lord has
given us that relate to our world, and not
on mysteries that have not been revealed to
us, may never be explained, or that just may
not be pertinent to our current circumstances.
Spiritual promptings and subtle impressions are
more common that one would suspect, however.
There are powerful intuitive communicators that
strongly influence us to push forward in the
direction of our dreams, toward a faith to
believe that will bless each of us with a
greater appreciation of where we
came from, why we are here,
and where we are going.

The
Devil was a liar
from the beginning.
Even now, He continues
his efforts to foil The Plan
of Salvation by the substitution
of his own counterfeit, unworkable
alternative that would have required
neither repentance nor the Atonement.
Fortunately, in a council setting in
heaven, we were able to see thru
his deception. Because of the
Holy Ghost, we still can
today.

When we turn our
backs to the invitation that has
been extended by the Holy Ghost to
reintroduce us to our Father in Heaven,
with Whom we were intimately associated
in the pre-earth existence, and we remain
alienated from Him by our spiritual death
because of our failure to embrace the
Atonement of His Son Jesus Christ,
it is unavoidable that we must
remain as hostages to our
natural inclinations that
are carnal, sensual,
and devilish.

Each time that
we follow up on the
righteous impressions we
receive from the Spirit, it is
as if we have re-established our
connection with God's perfect faith.
As we did in a pre-mortal classroom
setting that is but a distant memory,
we are once again blessed to sit
at His feet, as it were, to bask
in the light of His flawless
knowledge as well as
His unimpeachable
empathy.

Since
time immemorial,
the Spirit has blessed
us with the courge to take
calculated risks. And so, we
don't hesitate to break free from
the safety nets, the comfort zones,
and the ports of refuge to which the
timid apprehensively retreat at the
first sign of danger, to squeak
out their lives as they scurry
about from one shadowy
sanctuary to another,
in a flight from
faith.

While the Spirit encourages the development of personality traits that are in concordance with the symmetry of heaven, sin is harmful because it destroys our ability to nurture the equilibrium that is a defining characteristic of all those who inherit eternal life. It is in the nature of our Heavenly Father, His Son, and the Holy Ghost, that there is neither variableness, nor shadow of turning; nor indecisiveness, nor indecision.

The insolvency
of Satan's seduction
can only be abated by
a third-party bailout. The
sole solution to his nepotism
is to listen to the promptings of
our one true benefactor, Who is the
Holy Ghost. He is our silent partner,
and our institutional investor, our
venture capitalist, our pre-mortal
confidant, our faithful Pen-Pal,
and now our BFF.

The Holy Ghost has been our shepherd through the growing pains and mental, emotional, physical, and spiritual instability that are naturally related to early childhood development. Here on earth, because we age with the passage of time, we may think we have grown to adulthood, but He still envisions us as millennial children of God who continue to require His constant supervision.

Spiritual neglect
in any degree requires
that we take drastic action.
The plastic surgery of repentance
is prompted by the Holy Ghost, and is
indicated if we expect to experience a
reversal of our fortunes, and if we hope
to regain the likeness and image of
our Father, that was reflected in
our countenances throughout
our primeval childhood.

As
we venture
forth out of our
comfort zones and
we move forward with
purpose, we enlarge the
dimensions of our spiritual
center, to scribe a circle with
the stakes of Zion that provides
us with a glimpse of the magnitude
of our former home in heaven. Now,
with the uninterrupted intervention by
our Father in Heaven, His Son, and the
Holy Ghost, mortality can become
the wonderful learning center
for the talented and gifted
that it was envisioned to
be from before the
world was
made.

The
Spirit charges
our vision with an
infinite perspective,
where we experience the
pulsing stream of instinct,
insight, intuition, inspiration,
and revelation, whose flow can
be traced all the way back to their
source in heaven. To that end, we are
encouraged to give ourselves completely
and without reservation, that we might
enjoy a state of harmony with God,
and synchronization with eternity.
We search without ceasing, that
we might re-discover the
inherent power of
the Infinite.

William W. Phelps
realized that without the
Gospel, no-one "has found pure
space, nor seen the outside curtains,
where nothing has a place." Within the
roiling matrix of the temple, we realize
that there can be no end to matter, space,
spirit, or race; to virtue, might, wisdom, or
light; to union, youth, priesthood or truth;
to glory, love, or being. Our education
commences as we leave the waters of
baptism, when we embark upon a
path that leads back to our
divine center before holy
altars in the House
of the Lord.

The Spirit helps to reacquaint us with God's divine design as we put finishing touches on our dissertation on life. As we are perfected, our compositions will be recognized for what they have become. Each one of them is a true magnum opus that reflects God's work and glory. By inviting the Holy Ghost to release us from captivity, we are permitted to see things as they really are, and to enjoy lucidity that comes more from the heart than from the head. Thus, we are reminded of the peaceful setting back in our heavenly home, and of its instruction that so gently massaged our spirits.

The endowment soften our telestial tendencies and creates an impenetrable shield of faith. The Plan of Salvation, of which it testifies, provides a sounding board against which we may discern between the polarized opposites that seek our attention. The Atonement is its centerpiece, and it describes the differences between joy and its worldly counterfeits, and it strikes familiar chords within our heartstrings that remind us of our home back in heaven.

The Plan
of Salvation was
conceived in heaven,
but it envisioned our earthly
need to employ intrinsic counter
measures to wicked imaginations.
The noble character of those who
strive to live by its principles is
driven by altruism, self-denial,
self-discipline, self-restraint,
and self-sacrifice. These all
come as we listen with our
hearts to the promptings
of the Spirit that are as
the quiet whisper of a
gentle breeze that
caresses our
cheeks.

In harmony
with the principle
of opposition in all
things, an impenetrable
veil has been drawn across
our minds, shielding us from
eternity. But we have the Light
of Christ, and the unimpeachable
witness of the Holy Ghost, to assist us
in our efforts to probe that mysterious
curtain. In the interim, many of us are
swayed by the siren song of Satan, drawn
to the duplicitous shoals of his spiritual
instability, thereon to founder, and to
be pulled under water by the riptides
of religious relativism and by the
undertow of agnosticism, or by
faithless skepticism.

We can better
relate to the other
participants in life's
Three Act Play, and they
to us, if we see each other
against the milieu of the First,
Second, and Third Acts, namely,
our pre-earth life, mortality, and
life after death. Knowledge of this
sweeping panorama, of the intricacy,
complexity, and sophistication of the
Play itself, is explained during the
presentation of the endowment
in the House of The Lord.

Our attempts
to comprehend the
universe may help us
to understand ourselves.
If we ask, what is its origin,
or what is its ultimate destiny,
we are really asking where did we
come from, and where are we going.
When we discover the answers to these
questions, we will understand why we
are here, and we will be prepared to
embark upon a journey where our
traveling companion is the Holy
Ghost. With Him as our Guide,
we will find our way to a
pathway of faith into
the future.

Brigham Young taught that we will have revelation from the heavens to know our forefathers "clear back to Father Adam and Mother Eve, and we will enter into the temples of God and officiate for them." Then, we will be sealed to each other until the chain is made perfect all the way from the beginning of time, until its end, and we will be one happy family again.

With of the
restoration of guiding
principles and the doctrines
of the Gospel, the knowledge of
our origin and destiny is again made
available to all of the children of our
Heavenly Father, so much so, that in the
Last Days, our sons and our daughters
shall prophesy, our young men shall
have visions, and our old men
shall dream dreams.
(See Joel 2:28).

Wherever, whenever, and however we fit into the cosmos, we do know this: God quickens our lives, providing us with the animation of a physical world within which we freely interact with the Spirit. He "lends (us) breath, that (we) may live and move and do according to (our) own will, and (He supports us) from one moment to another." (Mosiah 2:21).

With
latter-day
revelation and
instruction in the
temple, we still only
dimly perceive our noble
heritage, and we sometimes
find it hard to accept the fact
that we mingled among the Gods
before our births. Our experiences at
the veil were envisioned from before
the foundation of the world; they were
to be molded in mortality but provide
a hint of eternity, as heaven smiles
upon us, and we are clothed in
the glory of God.

Some explain the intuition that we receive from the Holy Ghost as déjà vu, that literally means "already seen", in order to emotionally deal with the powerful impression that, somehow, a current event has already been experienced. Truly, religious recognition is just that, a re-cognition or a re-knowing of what we have already learned in our pre-mortal spiritual home.

The
decision
that was made
by our first parents
in the Garden to choose
the harder right instead of
the easier wrong, obviated the
'Progression Paradox' that had
faced them, wherein they would
have remained forever in "a state
of innocence, having no joy, for
they knew no misery; doing no
good, for they knew no sin."
(2 Nephi 2:23). Their choice
was anticipated before the
foundation of the world
by the Atonement
of Christ.

It was our Father Who
created the earth upon which we
stand as a learning laboratory, and
as a telestial testing center. It would
be a citadel of higher education, and a
home where we would be blessed to have
all of the tools that could conceivably
be necessary to validate His faith in
us; to see if we could muster an
equivalent faith in His Plan
for us, and to be proven
worthy of His trust.

The account of the Creation that was written by Moses provided only the details that relate to the Fall of Adam and Eve, and to the Atonement of Christ, which is the doctrine that we must understand in order to have the faith to be clean from the blood and sins of this generation, live life in abundance, and become heirs of salvation.

It must be with a great
deal of empathy that the Holy
Ghost shares our perspective, but
He also sees thru the clarifying and
purifying lens of eternity. He blesses
our lives in many ways by nurturing our
understanding of The Plan of Salvation.
The veil that has been drawn before our
eyes only prevents us, for a moment,
from seeing the wide expanse of
eternity from His unobstructed
viewpoint.

When
it is our time
to be reintroduced
to eternity, it will be
the Holy Ghost Who will
join in the transformation
of our mortal clay to a more
enduring substance. Our feelings
quietly whisper to us that we have
come to earth from a more exalted
sphere. The Spirit teaches that we are
God's chosen people, and that we live
within His embrace, enjoying a security
that others do not know. It blesses us
with a heavenly peace that surpasses
our understanding. We tingle with
the knowledge that we have been
called up and were chosen in
heaven, before we came to
dwell on the earth.

Because
of the influence
of the Holy Ghost,
both the heavens and
the earth are bathed in a
celestial fire that is akin to
the background radiation that
still lingers from the cataclysmic
moment of creation itself. The Holy
Ghost provides us with a stable star
map that defines the path that began
in the heavens, and that will lead us
all the way back to our pre-ordained
inheritance. He quite simply blesses
us with a promised endowment of
unearthly and radiant power.

We do not live in a Garden setting as did our first parents, but opposition still exists as the basis of a matrix of mayhem, within which the fiery darts of the adversary will trace an incendiary trail of disorder across an earthly sky. Only if we exhibit the moral discipline to respond to the steady guidance of the Holy Spirit, will we be able to recognize, address, reverse, and erase with finality, the imbalance in our lives. His nurturing influence will lead us back to the familiar stability of our heavenly home.

The disorder of life roughly jostles us further and further from the influence of the Spirit, whose purpose is to guide us away from that precipice of destruction, and to lead us homeward to a secure sanctuary where the stability of higher laws prevails. The temple teaches that we came into the world to die, but at the same time, thanks to the further light and knowledge that we receive in the revelatory nature of the endowment, we also learn about the Plan of Mercy that takes away the sting of death.

Standing in opposition to the Light of the Spirit is a darkness that has the potential to cover the earth, and gross darkness the people. Without the influence of the Holy Ghost to intervene in our behalf by reintroducing us to the Atonement that was promised from before the foundation of the world, we would forever be subject to the evil source of that darkness, to rise no more. The Spirit confirms our faith to see all the way back to heaven, and is quick to respond to our inquiry: "O God, where art thou, and where is the pavilion that covereth thy hiding place?" (D&C 121:1).

Our understanding
of the pre-mortal existence
as it unfolds in the endowment,
sanctifies life, dignifies individual
effort, and rewards achievement as
pivotal centers in God's perfect Plan
of Salvation. But even with the aid of
the most powerful telescopes known
to mankind, and notwithstanding
the Light of Christ, we have been
privileged only to take a peek
at the creations Moses beheld
through the power of faith
while under the mighty
influence of the
Spirit.

It we want to
complete the Gospel's course
curriculum, that we might graduate
graduate with honor from the school
of hard knocks, it surely must help to
have previously have given our language
to exhortation in the heavenly precincts of
pre-mortality. We have been anchored to the
infinite from the foundation of the world
through Gospel topsoil into a reservoir
of living water. Our repentance in this
life then becomes an expression of
our honesty with ourselves, with
our Father, with the Savior,
as well as with the
Holy Ghost.

We are baptized
because of our testimony
that the principles governing
the Fall of Adam, as well as the
Savior's Atonement, were "great and
eternal purposes (that) were prepared
from the foundation of the world."
(Alma 42:26). Our baptism itself
confirms that we understood
then, and now, the eternal
significance of the
sacrifice of our
Redeemer.

The Devil completely
misread the circumstances
surrounding the Fall of Adam,
and he misjudged the ability of
the Redeemer of the world to save
all of mankind thru the Atonement.
As it so happens, all that has been
necessary to restore purity in the
lone and dreary world is the
further light and knowledge
that God promised to give
us. The adversary never
even saw that one
coming.

In the temple,
in moments of deep
reflection as we soak in
the endowment, we learn that
we are begotten spirit children of
heavenly Parents, and that we lived
in our pre-mortal existence with Them
before we began our sojourn on earth.
We experience moments of dejá vu,
when with awakened memories we
realize that we are strangers on
earth, and have wandered
from a more exalted
sphere.

The Holy Ghost will
caress our spirits with
the inexplicable images of
religious recognition that will
remind us that we are of a noble
birthright. He is a light bearer Who
carries the torch of truth as a beacon
to guide us safely home. It makes no
difference how far or wide the net may
be cast, for science will never be able
to explain the flickering shadows of
eternity that dance around us. The
forgotten features of immortality
will once again be illuminated
for all to see, by the steady
light of the Spirit.

In the
scriptures, we are urged
129 times to learn, 154 times
to be perfect, and 306 times to
be obedient. But we are admonished
995 times to begin. Now is the time for
us to begin to re-establish our relationship
with the Holy Ghost, Who we knew so well in
our pre-mortal existence. Surely, He promised
us before we left home that He would be our
creative consultant as well as our guidance
counselor. Part of the reason why we chose
to come to earth must have been because
we knew He would always be available
to offer His constructive comments
relating to our developing
storyboard.

From before the foundation of the world, The Plan of God has been custom-designed to ultimately put each of us on trial, so that we might have our day in court. At the Bar of Justice, when we stand before Him on the Day of Judgement, our Father in Heaven will simply weigh the facts, and our previous acceptance or rejection of the Gospel, together with the Atonement, will determine our reward or our punishment. The legal proceedings have already been docketed to follow on the heels of our mortal experience, and we might be comforted to know that the Holy Ghost will be there to see that they will be carried out with impartiality.

Joseph Smith clearly understood where we came from, why we are here, and where we are going after we lay this mortal by. Just witness the dedicatory prayer he delivered at the Kirtland Temple: "Help us by the power of thy Spirit, that we may mingle our voices with those bright, shining seraphs around thy throne, with acclimations of praise, singing Hosanna to God and the Lamb." (D&C 109:79). He knew that The Plan had been designed that we might enjoy an unrestrained rapport with God. Its elements generate the power to "get things done" in an expansive and interactive way, in all holiness. When we follow its precepts, we will recognize His voice as the Spirit of truth, which "abideth and hath no end. And if it be in (us,) it shall abound." (D&C 88:66).

The account of the Creation that was recorded by Moses provided only the details that relate to the Fall of Adam and Eve, and to the Atonement of Christ, which is the doctrine that we must understand in order to have the faith to live abundantly and become heirs of salvation. In the scriptures, The Plan refers to worlds without number, but the application of its principles and doctrines relates only to the sphere upon which we live.

Both free will and
opposition are always before
us, and so the Spirit stands as
a sacred sentinel, beckoning us
to return to the easy familiarity of
heaven's gate, to find the Rest of God.
No matter that we are, for all intents
and purposes, dead weight, the Spirit
has the capacity to carry us until
we have been revitalized, and
can once again walk and
not be weary, and run
and not faint.

It may be
the Spirit that
causes our blood to
run hot, reminiscent of
the microwave background
radiation from the creation of
our universe billions of years ago,
as well as of the fiery cauldron of
experience that was catalyzed in
a garden setting eastward in
Eden, that was not so
very long ago.

When
we encounter
the true doctrine of
the Atonement of Jesus
Christ, our sinews resonate
with recognition. In this way,
every one has been blessed with
the innate capacity to hearken to
the voice of the Spirit, even the
Holy Ghost, that one day they
might return to the warm
embrace of their Father
Who waits for them
in heaven.

One of
life's purposes is
to refamiliarize us
with the noble principles
that guided us through the
spiritual kindergarten years of
our pre-mortal existence. We are
blessed with the companionship of
the Holy Ghost to accompany us
during our re-introduction to
that more natural state
of harmony with
heaven.

We persevere in our
obedience to our covenants
because of our testimony that
the doctrine relating to the Fall of
Adam, as well as to the Atonement of
Jesus Christ, reflects great and eternal
principles that predate the foundation
of the world. Our commitment may
be traced back to our baptism as
an ordinance that witnesses our
desire to immerse ourselves in
every ritual that has been
embedded within God's
great Plan of
Salvation.

Speaking to us from eternity, the Savior promised: I will go before your face. I will be on your right hand, and on your left, and my Spirit shall be in your hearts, and mine angels round about you, to bear you up." (D&C 84:88). With such assurance, how could we think to turn away from the Savior's Atonement by persisting in our wickedness, and by deceiving ourselves into believing that we can fly solo, without His parachute?

We have
been foreordained
in heaven before the world
was, to have glory added upon
our heads, on the condition of our
faithfulness to God, as we support Him
in His work by our actions. We are better
prepared to do so if we listen intently, as
the covenants of the temple are explained.
We open up our minds to options we have
never considered, envisioning a special
place called Kolob, signifying the
first creation, or the closest
body to the celestial, or
to the residence of
God.

Our attempts
to comprehend the
Atonement help us to
understand ourselves. It
is when we have discovered
the answers to where we came
from and why we are here that
we will be prepared to embark,
with unbounded confidence,
upon an incredible journey
of faith into our future,
to discover where we
are going.

Adam
and Eve fell that
they and their posterity
might be able to nurture the
moral fiber that we recognize
today as saving faith. They were
given the gift of the Holy Ghost,
to assist in their discovery of the
elusive equations of The Plan of
God, which had been prepared
from the foundation of the
world to be their guiding
theorems.

The Spirit of God selflessly moves us beyond dependence and even past independence, to a stimulating and interdependent relationship with Heavenly Father and Jesus Christ. As a facilitator, the Holy Ghost remains content to quietly but steadily remain behind the scenes to work in our behalf, as has been His inclination since time immemorial.

The Hubble
telescope can "see"
13.2 billion light years
into our past, almost to the
moment of creation itself, but
but it cannot gaze into heaven
for five minutes, which thing
the children of God love to
do, and which they do well,
when they have been cast
under the spell of
the Spirit.

Our
salvation
has less to do
with cherubim and
a flaming sword, and
more to do with our faith,
repentance, baptism, forgiveness
mercy, Atonement, the Sacrament,
and, ultimately, redemption. Because
of these doctrines, the Law of Mercy
trumps the Law of Justice through
forgiveness, and all is because
of the sacrifice of our Lord
and Savior, Jesus Christ
that was made from
before the world
was created.

It was through His
supernal demonstration of a
magnificent omniscience that our
Savior Jesus Christ negotiated with
Justice to execute the Law of Mercy.
Our Heavenly Father had beforehand
conceived the Atonement, in order
to bring about our metamorphosis.
We would not be condemned to
remain as fallen creations in a
cruel act of fate. We would
instead be transformed by
the power of heaven
into beings of
Light.

There will
come a day
for the faithful
when the sun shall
not go down, "neither
shall the moon withdraw
itself. For the Lord shall
be their everlasting light."
(See Isaiah 60:20). The Spirit
will re-introduce the children
of God to an unearthly light
that fills the immensity of
space because it emanates
all the way from their
heavenly home.

When we
feel the energy
of the Holy Ghost
building within us, we
realize that it can lift us
to the zenith of experience,
until the lines distinguishing
mortality from eternity blur.
At that moment, when we find
ourselves in a condition that,
for the lack of better words,
can only be described as if
we were being born again,
we will be consumed in
a fire of everlasting
burnings.

The endowment confirms that all who chose Heavenly Father's Plan in their pre-mortal life followed in the footsteps of Adam and Eve. In mortality, we will have opportunities to make similar choices; to be free to exercise our moral agency in ways that could not have been duplicated elsewhere.

The fire that was kindled on Sinai burned all the way from the earth "to the midst of heaven" itself. (Deuteronomy 4:11). Witnesses to this marvelous manifestation thought they could see thru a brilliant conduit into the depths of eternity itself. So it is, in the House of The Lord.

One of the basic messages of the Restoration is that Adam and Eve fell that they might have joy while on earth, as well as in heaven, thru repentance that, immediately after their expulsion from the Garden, was activated by their faith in the power of the Lord's Atonement to save them from their sins.

The
Atonement
looks right into
the jaws of spiritual
death without averting
its eyes. At the Council,
it was not the Savior, but
the Devil, who was the first
to blink. In consequence,
he was unceremoniously
cast out of heaven, a
fallen son of the
morning.

Forgiveness
of sins through
repentance is based
upon our understanding
of the Atonement, which is
why it surely formed the basis
of our pre-mortal classroom
curriculum. The initiative is
now ours, to experience
religious recognition,
or the re-knowing
of what we have
beforehand
learned.

We know by the casualty count from the ideological War in Heaven, that some of Heavenly Father's children forfeit their privilege to obtain a body. For those who remained faithful in the pre-earth existence, however, there came humbling liabilities, and so The Plan required the Creator to die for our sins, conditional only upon our heartfelt and sincere repentance.

The
Holy Ghost
nudges us off
our complacency
plateaus, as we steer
away from the trendy
cafés situated along the
broad avenues of Idumea.
We are lifted as on the wings
of eagles, beyond the detours of
our self-imposed limitations, back
on to the familiar highway that had
aforetime guided us from heaven,
for our foreordained rendezvous
with destiny, right here
on the earth.

It is not enough merely to have received the gift of the Holy Ghost. If we coast to a standstill before we have made our way to the feet of our Savior Jesus Christ, we are at risk of toppling over. We need forward momentum to maintain the heavenly balance that was taught to us when we were toddlers in our spiritual kindergarten, so that when we finally take off our training wheels after the conclusion of our mortal experience, we will be able to joyfully whiz right thru the pearly gates of heaven.

The spiritual sixth sense that blesses us with the memory of our noble heritage may just be the lowest common denominator in a theory of everything. The influence of the Holy Ghost is a grand unifying phenomenon, and although it exists without dispute, it defies explanation on a chalkboard, as well as within the algorithms of any mathematical equation.

The
Atonement
links the riches
of eternity with the
resources of the earth.
But those who disregard
the former because they are
obsessed by the latter, will be
doomed to live out their lives in
scarcity of their basic spiritual
needs. They will live beneath
the poverty level without
even being aware
of it.

By
the Spirit,
we are caught
up in a rapture
where we can almost
hear legions of angels
who confirm that the earth
was designed from before its
foundation to be "a machine for
the making of gods." (Henri Bergson).
Because we are strangers from a realm
of light who have forgotten all, we must
listen to the Spirit, to learn why we're
here, and who we really are. As we
do so, the stage is set for the
reawakening of magical
memories.

It makes
no difference
to our Father in
Heaven whether it is
the influences of the
Seven Deadly Sins, or the
garden-variety transgressions
that we commit every day, that
we are combatting. The Holy Ghost
will always be there to guide us
back to the spiritual center of
our heavenly home, from
which we have strayed.

The Spirit will introduce us to a ladder that has been set up on the earth, the top of which reaches all the way back to heaven. No matter in which direction it faces, we will always feel the presence of the Holy Ghost as He abides before us in the past, present, and future.

The
Holy Ghost
will inexorably
draw us closer to
the Divine Center of
Beings Who inhabit a more
exalted sphere. Our communion
with the Infinite will cause us to
shrink from sin, and to think of it
as repulsive. The Spirit will envelop us
in an intuitive appreciation of where we
came from, the tangible element of why we
are here, and the revelatory reassurance
of where we are going.

The
great and eternal
purposes of God have
been dramatically articulated
within a legally binding endowment
that has been prepared from before the
foundation of the world. It addresses our
utilization of a spiritual currency whose value
is sufficient to purchase our souls. It is only by
the power of the Holy Ghost, Who acts as our
fund manager, that we are able to make
sense of this celestial document as its
terms are explained to us. He blesses
us with revelation to stir us with
sweet remembering, and with
a desire to return to our
home in heaven.

It is by the
power of the Spirit
that we fondly remember
our 'happy place' in heaven.
In our hearts, we return to the
magical kingdom of our childhood,
to re-discover that special place where
dreams come true. As we are carried aloft,
we are invited to take the second star on the
right and continue straight on 'til morning; we
move beyond our spatial, temporal, and even
spiritual limitations, to experience the
enchanting influence of the Holy
Ghost, Who, as it turns out, is
our Best Friend Forever.

Those
who zip along
in the fast lane of
life can far too easily
blow right past the celestial
signposts that have been erected
by the Holy Ghost, that would have
alerted them to move over, to take
an exit that would have guided
them back to the security
of familiar territory
near heaven's
gate.

It is with
the eye of faith
and from the vantage
point of the eternal world
from which we have so recently
departed, that we are privileged to
see more clearly. It is as if we have
somehow escaped our mortal clay
with all its confining limitations
that distort our perspective
and negatively twist our
attention inward, to
worldliness.

The Holy Ghost has the highest level of security clearance, that allows Him to browse through our applications, and then to restore to its default settings the spiritual appestat that is a critical design feature of our mortal bodies. In particular, He does this when He notices that we are indulging, and even binge eating, in sin.

As we repent, we draw upon the magnificent power of all three members of the Godhead, so that we may become increasingly receptive to flashes of insight. We are cast off into streams of revelation that carry us along in quickening currents that re-introduce us to direct experience with Father in Heaven, with Jesus Christ and with the Holy Ghost.

We
who seek the
influence of the
Holy Ghost want to
be pure in heart, that
we might enjoy intrinsic
countermeasures to wicked
imaginations. Our behavior is
driven by altruism, self-denial,
self-discipline, self-restraint,
and self-sacrifice. These all
come as we listen with our
hearts to the promptings
of the Spirit that bring
us to a remembrance
of our former
home.

As we learn to
listen in moments of quiet
reflection to the whisperings of
the Spirit, we increase our capacity
to look beyond the temptations of
temporal trivia. We develop a will
to adjust our perspective, so that
we can see more distinctly that
the pillars of creation, our
very foundations, have
been constructed
elsewhere.

Agency and opposition are powerful forces that refine us as they push, pull, and tear away at us in the crucible of experience. On our own, we cannot eliminate the consequences when we fall short of perfection in our efforts. For that to happen, our Heavenly Father provided us with the Redeemer of Israel, even the Lamb slain from the foundation of the world.

Faith is dead, without the accompanying work of repentance that is made possible by the Atonement. Even great faith lacks the power to save us from the unalterable demands of Justice. So that Mercy might prevail, from the beginning God provided us with a Mediator, as well as with the Holy Ghost.

Without the sweet, sustaining influence of the Holy Ghost, we are inclined to seek after signs. When we are past feeling, we need greater and greater intensities of stimulation to receive the same levels of temporal or theological gratification. Although we may unconsciously yearn for the light of our former home in heaven, what we have been given never seems to be enough.

We are here
to train our lips to
articulate only positive
expressions of speech and
to never speak guile, and our
shoulders to develop the strength
to bear the burdens of those who
have been battered and bruised
by the vicissitudes of life and
who may be faltering under
the heavy weight of sorrow
or unresolved sin.

Why are we here?

As a community of Saints who are living within the household of faith, we are unified, even as The Plan recognizes our diversity. It quickly moves us away from dependence and independence, to interdependence. However, it blesses us with a solid conformity without asking that we give up our individuality or those things that make us unique. It invites us to prostrate ourselves in the supplication of His grace before His mighty throne, and to partake of His goodness. For He will deny none that come unto Him, whether they be black or white, in chains or free, male or female, and He remembers the heathen; and all are alike unto God, both Jew and Gentile. (See 2 Nephi 26:33).

The golden
cobblestones of a
pathway to the stars are
illuminated by the principles
of true conversion. These guide
us in the direction of the recognition
of our iniquity, and then to a deep godly
sorrow for our sins. Next comes inescapable
suffering and torment that stimulates an appeal
to the Savior, with an awakening understanding
of the Atonement. After our baptism, comes the
remission of our sins, spiritual enlightenment,
and great joy. This motivates us to pursue a
lifestyle of righteousness and service that
is punctuated by our weekly observance
of the Sacrament of the Lord's Supper.
Each time this occurs, the endless
loop cycles one more time, but
it is calibrated to a higher
plane of spiritual
awareness.

Even as we
make valiant efforts
to focus the powers of our
intellect on eternal elements,
because we are bounded on all
sides by a crushing present reality,
if our hearts have not been softened
to relate to the things of the Spirit, we
cannot understand the creations of God
except in the most academic, abstract, and
obtuse ways. Joseph Smith explained that we
must have a change of heart if we wish to
see the kingdom of God. Mortality is a
schoolmaster that mentors us, that our
hearts might become as pliable clay
in the hands of the Master Potter.
We are lucky to be blessed with
the gift of the Holy Ghost,
and to be witnesses
of His power.

During the genesis of our faith, it is necessary for us to take a few steps into the darkness, that we might allow the spiritual strong searchlight of truth to illuminate the way. Only after the trial of our faith, will it be confirmed by the Spirit that the Savior is both its Author and Finisher. He has us covered coming and going. But if we permit ourselves to succumb to fear, and allow faithlessness to handcuff the expression of our trust, often all that is left in the end is a monochromatic and one-dimensional compromise that leaves us with a hollow core of emptiness in the pit of our stomachs and terror in our hearts. When faith says its prayers, it asks for intercession by the Spirit.

After the Flood, the
ancients built ziggurats
that were simply towers that
had been specifically designed
to reach all the way into heaven.
The Tower of Babel is an example of
these exaggerated temple spires. However,
their designers and builders, and those who
flocked to behold their architectural marvels,
missed the point. Instead of creating physical
structures composed of nothing more than
brick and mortar, they could have more
profitably spent their time by using the
principles taught by The Plan of God
to build enduring relationships
with each other and with Him
with the material of
saving faith.

The covenants we make with God provide us with unequivocal understanding, as well as with unambiguous definitions of eternal truth. They provide ways for us to be taught by the events within which we are swept up, to learn from our relationships with others, and to grow within our environment no matter how unique or difficult it might seem. They protect us from the worldly influences that continually encroach upon the fortress of our spiritual symmetry. Our covenants are as celestial thermostats that can easily mitigate the mercurial volatility of the telestial tempests that rage over the landscapes of our lives.

We keep our eyes
fixed on the prize, as we
reach out beyond our comfort
zones to snatch the golden rings
that tantalize us as they dangle beside
the carousels of life. The resourcefulness
and originality of the mind and the will of
God are such that the execution of The Plan
was designed with redundant mechanisms that
would provide us with repetitive opportunities
to pause for analysis, reflection, commitment,
and renewal, while miraculously minimizing
our tendency to focus inward. As our lives
conform to its principles, we find our
greatest expression, and self-doubt,
second-guessing, and back
pedaling are virtually
eliminated.

The
light of
the Spirit gives
the threads in the
fabric of our faith a
a vivacity unique to holy
vestments. Their steadfast
colors will never fade, except
through neglect. They will remain
impervious to every blemish save the
stubborn stains of unresolved sin. It is
as if our covenants are speaking to us,
repeatedly asking if we have embraced the
moral element of responsibility which is the
companion of knowledge, or if we possess the
spiritual and the intellectual maturity to handle
experience with accountability. When we dare to
grapple with these interrogatives, we come to an
epiphany, as we determine to do our best to be
righteous stewards of the power that has been
vested in us by God, through all generations
of time and throughout all eternity.

So
much power
has been vested
in the Atonement of
of Christ, that even if we
have been gravely wounded
by our sins, they will not heal
imperfectly, leaving soul scars.
Thru the application of the Balm
of Gilead, the adhesions that are
the result of telestial trauma will
very quickly fade away, leaving no
trace of damage. Telestial E.M.T.s
seemingly leave no stone unturned
as they look around for diagnosis,
but it is only the Gospel of Jesus
Christ that can provide a virtual
war chest of therapies for cold,
stony, and hard hearts. Faith
is the remedy of choice for
reconciliation with the
heavens.

We may
be very surprised
to find that the purpose
of our lives simply involves
the mastery of two principles:
Our own repentance, as well as our
forgiveness of the trespasses by others.
When we are permitted to look with the
eye of faith thru a spiritual prism, we can
see beyond the limited horizon of our sight,
all the way into eternity. Our eyes are opened
by the Spirit to understand the things of God.
The evidence of the absolute genius behind The
Plan of God is that it turns our thoughts to the
Spirit, to our covenants, to the Savior, to His
Atonement, and to the commandments. It
is discipline that expands the capacity
of our understanding to reveal that,
as far as forgiveness is concerned,
the door swings both ways, and
life can be greater than the
sum of its parts.

In the heavens
before the world was made,
it was apparent that something
would need to be done in order to
counteract the unforgiving reality check
of our birth. To that end, Heavenly Father
has instilled within us the instinctive desire to
enjoy bonds with each other that can transcend
physical relationships. He has stamped each of our
hearts with a blueprint for our survival. He planted
within its instruction the insight and intuition we
would need to organize ourselves and prepare
every needful thing, so that we might establish
houses of prayer, fasting, faith, learning,
glory, and order; even houses of God
where dreams come true, and where
we all live happily ever after.
(See D&C 109:8).

We only learn
by personal experience
that the greatest miracle
is not raising the physically
dead, but healing the spiritually
sick. A hand picked trauma team
with specialty training in advanced
spiritual life support techniques stands
ready to attend to our needs. They draw
upon the virtue of The Plan of God, and
its ability to touch our hearts, to change
our nature, to soften us and to humble
us, to make us as pliant clay in the
hands of the Master Potter, to mold
us as children, and to securely
envelop us in the happiness
that has been prepared
for the Saints.

Disciples of Christ take commitment to a new level. They redefine dedication. They exercise their duties in ways that are truly selfless. The Gospel has transformed their lives. They are as the people of Zarahemla, who declared to King Benjamin: "The Spirit of the Lord Omnipotent ... has wrought a mighty change in us, or in our hearts, that we have no more disposition to do evil, but (instead) to do good continually." (Mosiah 5:2).

We left
our home in heaven
to come to this earth,
to become acquainted with
evil as well as with good, with
pain as well as with pleasure, and
with darkness as well as with light;
with error as well as with truth, and
with punishment for the infraction of
God's eternal laws, as well as with the
blessings that follow our obedience.
Only the Atonement of Jesus Christ
makes it possible for us to turn
the opposition we all face into
character-building life
experiences.

In one of the more memorable episodes of "Star Trek", Captain Picard asks Q: "What is it you're trying to tell me?" To which omnipotent and omniscient Q replies: "You'll find out!" So it is, as we engage our journey through mortality. The air in the theater of life is charged as fire in the sky, with an electricity that merges the universal encouragement of the Light of Christ with the pointed and providential guidance of the Holy Ghost, as we discover for ourselves the unknown possibilities of existence.

When we walk in
the light of life and
we go out of our way to
grasp the principles of truth,
we brim over with gratitude as
we explore our accommodations in
the household of faith, discovering that
they offer unobstructed views of the Holy
Ghost. We realize that when God unveiled
our world, and said: "Let there be light!" it
was a simple statement of fact as much as
it was a command. It was His invitation
to us to recognize, embrace, and to
celebrate the celestial energy that
is dancing all around us in a
revelatory rapture.

Our temple covenants are as chiropractic adjustments that we receive to treat our spiritual scoliosis. The sturdiest plants, and those that bear the best fruit, are those that have deep roots in good, rich, nurturing soil. The endowment teaches us to integrate ourselves into a loam that is rich in art, courtesy, decency, example, honor, music, and virtue. Its object is to allow our spirits to grow freely, beyond narrow confines that are the equivalent of one-pint nursery containers. We send down taproots into that soil which is the Gospel, and thereby we anchor ourselves to the Infinite.

Standing in
unspoken opposition to the
grace of God is a darkness that is
so pervasive that it has the potential
to cover the earth, and gross darkness
the people. Without repentance, baptism,
and the Atonement of Christ, we would
be blinded by the evil source of that
melancholy and left destitute; to
hesitantly tap our way through
life, bereft of the power to
triumphantly rise in the
resurrection of the
just with the
Saints of
God.

To some
degree, we find
ourselves susceptible
to the influences of the
Seven Deadly Sins. In every
case, however, the Atonement
of Christ stands ready to rescue
us. Repentance rekindles our zest
for life by reviving our enthusiasm,
restoring our divine inspiration, and
by recalibrating the celestial compass
that rests within our beating hearts,
which the Spirit reminds us is, as
it were, a burning within
our bosom.

Temple covenants are life-generating and life-sustaining, for just as we are "born into the world by water, and blood, and the spirit" and have become of dust living souls, even so, we "must be born again into the kingdom of heaven, of water, and of the Spirit, and be cleansed by blood," even the blood of the Son of God, and receive our endowment in the temple, that we "might be sanctified from all sin, and enjoy the words of eternal life in this world, and eternal life in the world to come, even immortal glory." (Moses 6:59-60).

It may be that
the most significant
difference that explains the
superiority of the principles of The
Plan of Salvation over other lifestyles,
is the process whereby the Gospel of Jesus
Christ is internalized by His disciples. The
wonder of our transformation begins with
sanctification by the Spirit at the waters
of baptism, and continues when we
participate in the ordinances of
exaltation that are carried
out before holy altars
in the House of
the Lord.

Faith, light, and truth may be recognized as irreducible common denominators. These are the essential elements of an equation that describes the foundation upon which we receive knowledge. "One for all, and all for one!" was the ringing motto of the Three Musketeers. Without the Athos of faith, the Porthos of light, and the Aramis of truth, we would lose knowledge. We would degenerate from God and descend to the devil. Without the guidance of the Spirit to be with us, we cannot be saved.

It is
not God's
intention to
give us a second
wind in the first mile
of the race, when we have
only just begun our journey.
When we are caught up in the
trauma of temporal traps, because
we have allowed our faith to become
so flawed that we have been blinded to
the impotence of our false gods, sooner
or later, the misery that we have created
will catch up to us. At the end of the day,
we will all need God's power to give us
renewed bursts of energy. Without it, we
must remain confused, disillusioned,
abandoned or despairing as a
result of our focus on the
pleasures of the world,
and we will perish
in Babylon.

We have come to
our earthly homes to
learn what the prototypical
family looks like. Under ideal
circumstances, they prepare us to
become the parents we want to be.
They are the corporeal embodiment of
training manuals whose working models
teach us about the celestial principles of
service, sacrifice, and consecration. They
teach us about the four cardinal virtues
of prudence, temperance, fortitude, and
justice, and about the three heavenly
graces of faith, hope, and charity.
They teach us how we can learn
to love ourselves and each
other, and to be moral,
accountable, and
responsible.

As long as we remain in a state of rebellion against the Spirit, the fruit of the Tree of Life must remain just beyond our reach, even if, for the sake of curiosity, we now and then would like to take a bite. If we never raise our eyes to search eternal horizons, the world before us will appear as nothing more than a barren desert that is devoid of refreshing oases, the welcome shade of trees, and an abundance of well watered gardens. If we lack faith to nourish the word, not even its living water can sustain us.

The
Holy Ghost
encourages us
to constantly strive
to do more, to be better,
to seek understanding, and
to empower ourselves with the
blessing of wisdom. We emulate
the Olympic motto, which is "Citius,
Altius, Fortius," or "Faster, Higher," and
"Stronger." Among the greatest virtues with
which we can be blessed are a well-trained
mind and a body to match, the happiness
that comes from achievement, and the
influence of the Spirit. If we lack
these, our lives are nothing but
smoke and mirrors, and we
grow old before our
time.

After the Fall, the
portal to Eden may have swung
shut, but as it did so, another door
opened that introduced Adam and Eve
to a secret garden accessible only to those
who would utilize the key of the Atonement,
thru baptism by immersion for the remission of
their sins. They would be able to have successful
outcomes with the good as well as with evil, with
virtue as well as with vice, with health as well
as with sickness, with pleasure as well as
with pain, and with light as well as
with darkness, in the white-hot
crucible of experience.

The Atonement of Christ
commits us to the arduous process
of choosing the harder right, that is
accompanied by a spiritual rebirth. Its
alternative would leave us to follow a
wobbly course that leads to the easier
wrong. But that is a devilish detour
that is characterized by the desire
to subvert The Plan of God by
forcing the capitulation by
Mercy to the miscarriage
of Justice, wherein we
would somehow be
saved in our
sins.

When the Law of Justice
has been reconciled with Mercy,
the Atonement and our repentance
make The Plan perfect. They allow the
worst of us to work out our salvation with
fear and trembling before the Lord, as we
earn the privilege, as prodigal sons and
daughters of a Father Who loves us, to
rejoin His household of faith in full
fellowship, with all the privileges
one might hope for, subject to
the reformation of errant
behavior and flawed
character.

The
Holy Ghost is our
mentor and our teacher.
If we are good students and
we have turned in our homework,
Gospel principles will illuminate our
minds and our spirits. We will be bathed
in a cascade of insight, intuition, inspiration
and revelation. He will remind us to be patient
in the face of challenges when the proportion
of the problems looming before us seems
daunting, when our difficulties seem
unreasonable, or if our portion
seems unfair.

In the Spirit World, the departed are taught the Gospel of Jesus Christ. Those who accept it there need to have the ordinances performed in their behalf by "saviors (who) shall come up on mount Zion." (Obadiah 1:21). The Saints are "set to be a light unto the world, and to be the saviors of men," as they make the journey to the temples of the Lord, primarily to do work for those who have not the means to do it for themselves. (D&C 103:9).

In the temple, we interact with members of the Church who grapple with their own custom-tailored challenges, but who have somehow made the transition from hesitancy to conviction, from instability to commitment, from timidity to confidence, from indecision to resolution, from doubt to certainty, from struggle to celebration, and from vacillation to purpose. In short, they have moved beyond spiritual itinerancy to moral discipline.

Since
the testimony
of Jesus Christ is
the spirit of prophecy,
the Holy Ghost becomes a
facilitator who helps to bring
others of God's children to the
knowledge of His Plan, and to their
own independent witness of the Savior.
The progress we make in life centers on
what we do with the Atonement of Jesus
Christ and upon what His Gospel does
for us. Ideally, they will create
a connection of understanding
with the ability to bridge the
gap that would otherwise
exist between heaven
and earth.

Our
obstacles
are frightful
things we see when
we take our minds off
our goals. They loom large
with gratuitous significance. The
Spirit endows us with the vision to
see beyond these potential stumbling
blocks. It empowers us to rely upon the
expansive and creative engine for positive
change that is driven by the Holy Ghost.
We turn the boulders that loom large
in our lives into stepping-stones
that pave the way to higher
achievement.

The activities in which the unfaithful are engaged do not require commitment to a belief, but only minimal effort, little responsibility, and virtually no accountability. Someone once said that the Lord gave us two ends; one to think with and the other to sit on. Which one we use will determine how well we do in life. In other words: Heads we win, and tails we lose. But it's always nice to have a little help from our friends, beginning with our greatest advocate, our Savior Jesus Christ.

It seems only natural that our Father in Heaven would want to maintain a correspondence with His children who have left their heavenly home to embark upon a mortal mission, and so He continues to reveal many great and important things pertaining to our lives here on the earth. He sends us tenderly composed "letters" of encouragement hoping that we will receive and read them with excitement. Open lines of communication from the Spirit are nurtured to become avenues of correspondence that freely flow between heaven and earth.

Each one of us
has been placed on the
earth that we might attend the
temple, which has been consecrated
to be a revelatory observatory. When
we look up at the stars, we are able to
see things as they really are, through the
clarifying lens of eternity. The aura within
the House of the Lord is crystal clear, and
its uncontaminated atmosphere blesses us
to be able to discern between right and
wrong and good and evil; in short, to
make prudent choices that are based
upon celestial certainties, without
the distortion of even a hint
of telestial pollution.

One of the terrible
consequences of the
world's fascination with
Babylon, and of its adoption
of the lifestyle of Beelzebub, is
spiritual insensitivity that is born
of competition between individuals.
Win or lose is the prevailing standard.
Zero sum game is the rule of play. While
business teaches that we don't get what we
deserve; we get what we negotiate, in the
Plan of God we realize that appeasement,
mediation, concession, compromise, and
arbitration are conspicuously absent.
We only see the work and glory
of God in action. We see
religion that is pure
and undefiled.

Standing out
in sharp contrast
to the frenzied demands
that are thrust upon us by the
world, The Plan of God generates
many opportunities during our journey
home for us to stop what we are doing, that
we might smell the roses. In fact, it was in a
Garden setting that our Heavenly Father created
fruits and flowers of every description, as love
letters to His children. (See Genesis 1:11). The
poet wrote of these delicate reinforcements:
"Earth is crammed with heaven, and every
bush with fire of God. But only those
who see, take off their shoes. The
rest stand around picking
blackberries."

If we are ever to obtain our exaltation of eternal life, we must do more than simply acknowledge that Jesus Christ is Lord. Temple ordinances make it abundantly clear that the critical point of conversion, beyond which lie the encircling flames of fire in the Celestial Kingdom of God, rests in making the conscious decision to accept not only Jesus Christ, but also to be obedient to His commandments. These necessarily include the covenants we make before God, angels, and witnesses before holy altars in the House of the Lord.

Those who eagerly embrace the Atonement of Jesus Christ embark upon a journey that is as old as time. Their faith will introduce them to a procedure with which they may not be familiar, even that of a spiritual heart transplant. As they face a bright future after they have been born again in a newness of life, carefully prescribed anti-rejection protocols need to be followed, in order to protect and preserve the new organ that is steadily beating in their chests.

Our greater
understanding of
The Plan of Salvation
that is revealed in the
House of the Lord blesses
our lives in many ways. Its
power creates the opportunity
for dynamic change, as wisdom
flows along established channels.
Moreover, personal accountability,
responsibility, and commitment to
obedience expand. A humble need
to serve strengthens the bonds of
brotherhood and sisterhood, and
generates interdependency in a
community of true believers in
which any cultural boundaries
are effectively expunged. We
are no more strangers or
foreigners, but become
fellowcitizens with
the Saints in the
household of
God.

God's Plan was designed as a locomotive to help us to enjoy our ride through life. We climb aboard a train bound for glory. We have a first-class ticket, so that the dust, delays, sidetracks, smoke, cinders, and jolts will be a lot more comfortable. Our conductor on that train is Jesus Christ, Who provides significant relief from the pressures of the journey, by punching our tickets with His Atonement.

The Holy Ghost proves that darkness cannot penetrate a brightly illuminated chamber, and so we seize every opportunity we can to be enveloped in light. We have learned to face the sunshine, so the shadows will always be behind us. Darkness will still exist, but its companions that take the form of fear and uncertainty will be out of sight, out of mind, and out of luck. They cannot harm us as long as we have the Spirit to be with us.
(See D&C 20:77)

Secular humanism and other ideologies that extoll the virtues of the intellect and demand tangible proof are incompatible with the Holy Ghost. They destroy faith, and divert us from following The Plan whose successful execution hinges upon nourishing the seeds of innocent faith in the revealed word of God. Speaking of those who would denigrate the Bible, Sir Walter Scott wrote: "Better had they ne'er been born, who reads to doubt, or reads to scorn."

As imperfect
mortals who are
struggling to believe
what we do not see, the
reward of our maturing faith
is to see what we believe. Some
things just have to be believed to
be seen. Then, when our emerging
faith has been transformed by our
experience, we can say, as did the
believing man who had been blind
from his birth, but was healed by
the Light of Life: "One thing I
know, whereas I was blind,
now I see." (John 9:25).

In
order for
it to function
optimally, The Plan
requires that we take
God's labor of love and
somehow ease onto a world
stage that is lit only by fire.
The ordinances of the House of
the Lord amplify our yearning to
come inside out of the cold, and to
reach that most holy faith that was
envisioned by Heavenly Father, that
a comfortable connection with the
Holy Ghost might be created, as
well as a warm relationship
with heaven itself.

We live in the
midst of Spiritual Babylon,
and recoil as we encounter the
sprawling wasteland of worldliness
that reeks of the rotting stench of sin.
The Holy Ghost cannot be dragged down
to its level, however, for He would never
allow Himself to be contaminated by the
raw sewage unleashed by the servants
of Satan, who sometimes attempt to
disguise themselves as sanitation
workers who think their sole
mission in life is to save
us from ourselves.

As
cast members of
Life's Three Act Play,
we can better understand
our roles if we have engaged
others in the scenes we play. We
need to be on familiar terms with
those who participate in the drama,
and share the stage with them as we
rehearse how we might deal with the
challenges we face that are related
to mastering the assignments that
are unique to each of our
individual parts.

Our faith
in the divine Plan
of our Father in Heaven
is confirmed in the temple,
where we learn that it has been
designed to bring us back into His
presence after we have grown up unto
the Lord to discover that the basis of a
hope of salvation is in His Atonement. In
the temple, our telestial tendencies are
transformed into celestial sureties in
a process of generation. Without the
life-generating ordinance of the
endowment, it could be argued
that we cannot really be
born again.

It is
our destiny to
see the righteousness
of our labors revealed
in spectacular simplicity
and plainness. The walls of
opposition to our purposeful
repentance will crumble and
fall away. In our efforts, the
Lord will comfort and succor
us with the Bread of Life. As we
journey through the harsh and
unforgiving wastelands of
Babylon, seeking the Lord
while He may be found,
oases will spring up
in the desert and
living water will
slake our
thirst.

It is nothing less than the unblemished innocence, simplicity, transparency, purity, and virtue of little children who are about to be baptized that blesses us with the optimism that the peace of God is within our reach. When we change our nature to be as they are, that is humble, meek, submissive, patient, and full of love, it will be the enticings of the Holy Spirit that will help us to fulfil our destiny, to put off our natural inclinations, and become as Saints. Although we may be adults, we can become as little children, thru the infinite and eternal Atonement of Christ.

From the
liberating and
refreshing perspective
of Mercy, the Savior of the
world has negotiated with Justice
to purchase our sins with the legally
recognized currency of the Atonement.
His voluntary act of sacrifice is perfectly
balanced and attuned to accomplish the
task at hand, but it is augmented by
faith, repentance, baptism, the Gift
of the Holy Ghost, and finally,
by the Sacrament, all of which
are principles, doctrines,
and ordinances that
lends support to
God's mission
statement.

It is in this life
that we must prepare for
our reunion with our Father
in Heaven, by striving to become
pure and holy. As we seek the Spirit,
our participation in the Sacrament is
the tangible expression of our appeal
to the Savior to come to our rescue.
In particular, it reflects our faith
in His Atonement to heal the self
inflicted damage that has been
caused by sin, that can be the
result of weakness in the
integrity of the armour
of our shields of
faith.

The Holy Ghost is
the best fitness trainer
we could ever have. But His
performance requirements do
ask us to expend soul-sweat. As
Robert Frost reflected: "I shall be
telling this with a sigh somewhere
ages and ages hence: Two roads
diverged in a wood, and I took
the one less traveled by, and
that has made all the
difference."

Belief may be the mental assent to the actuality of a precept or principle, but it lacks the moral element of responsibility that we call faith. Of those to whom much is given, however, much is expected. The gift of faith demands action that is shared between ourselves and the Holy Ghost. When His witness is balanced with our faith to believe, our works will naturally reflect our new-found zeal.

With our faith
to choose the harder
right, while distaining the
easier wrong, we will avoid
the world's amusement parks,
and will gratefully utilize the
aid station of the Atonement
that has been providentially
positioned in Zion. We will
use the Savior's sacrifice
as a celestial barometer
that is calibrated to a
scale that measures
the capacity of
our hearts.

Through
the Atonement of
Jesus Christ, we are
exposed to a constant
flow of insight, intuition,
inspiration, and revelation
that simply streams forth in a
downpour of divine direction.
It blesses us as we walk along
illuminated pathways and as we
exercise our faculties of mind
and spirit. The Plan leads us
to the community of Christ,
so that, together, we may
enjoy divine direction
in the household
of faith.

We have
come to earth to
make covenants with
God in the House of The
Lord. These were not just
designed that we might live
as families forever. They were
also created to teach us how to
live now, how to appreciate the
dominion enjoyed by God, how
to use the tools He has given to
us, and how to create a heaven
on earth where we may retain
a hope of eternal life, even
as we vigorously engage
mortality. Carpe
diem!

Temple experiences, culminating in the endowment, have real meaning only to those who have accepted God and Christ, have entered the fold thru the covenant of baptism, and have received the Holy Ghost. These are they who have made a conscious determination to serve God and enter into a covenant relationship with Him. Doing so prepares them to endure to the end of their lives in righteousness.

The
Atonement
permits us to
free ourselves
from the mire of
sin, and to cleanse
ourselves in the blood
of Jesus Christ; to stand
steadily upon Gospel sod.
Our faith separates us from
those who precariously hop
about on the flotsam and
the jetsam that bob up
and down, and toss
to and fro, on the
unpredictably
roily seas
of life.

We are
lucky to have
been blessed with
faith in the Atonement
of Christ, and to become
witnesses of His power. We
are sanctified in Him by the
grace of God, and through
the shedding of His blood,
which is in the covenant
of His Father, unto the
remission of our sins.
We are consecrated
to become holy
and without
spot.

There is an
ever-present
negative energy
that can influence
our affairs, and the
Atonement is its only
viable countermeasure.
Its sole stipulations are
that we confess when we
have, in any magnitude,
embraced the opposites
that lie before us, and
that we unhesitantly
instigate the safety
protocols required
by repentance to
convey us back
into harmony
with heaven.

Our faith may as well be dead, without the accompanying work of repentance that is made possible by the Atonement, and continually fortified as we partake of the Sacrament. Our faith notwithstanding, we do not have the power to save ourselves from the unalterable demands of Justice. So Mercy might flourish, our Heavenly Father created covenants so that existence would have meaning and purpose as our lives were bound to His ordinances of not only salvation but also exaltation.

Those with
the faith to choose
the harder right are like
"brave Horatius, the Captain
of the Gate," who declared: "To
each of us upon this earth, death
cometh soon or late. And how can
we die better, than facing fearful
odds, for the ashes of our fathers
and the temples of our gods?"
Here was a man who trusted
his relationship with
the Spirit.

In every age,
the tender shoots of
young testimony spring up
and are carefully nurtured in
accordance with Alma's inspired
formula. Our understanding comes
from the Spirit of Truth, without the
ecclesiastical embroidery that too
often needlessly complicates the
simple sewing, and sowing, of
Gospel doctrine and its
related principles.

It is only
after we have caught
the Spirit of the Holy Ghost
that the depth and breadth of
our comprehension finally puts to
rest the debates that have preoccupied
man since the beginning of the Age of
Reason. We soar to new heights in the
dawning Age of Enlightenment, as the
reconciliation between science and
religion harmonizes and clarifies
our understanding of our place
both in the universe and in
the eternities.

We have come
to earth "like gentle rain
through darkened skies," with
the anticipation of receiving the
image of God in our countenances, so
that our faces will reflect an unearthly
light, as we are transformed from within.
The world seeks change from the outside,
and fails miserably. The Gospel, on the
other hand, changes us from the inside,
and succeeds brilliantly. We are thus
created to reach our potential in
both the image and likeness
of God our Father.

Even as it
teaches basic economic,
social, behavioral, political
and earth sciences, the temple
endowment does so in creative ways
that are alien to the understanding of
Spiritual Babylon. It is where we go, to
paraphrase King Benjamin, to open our
ears, so that we might hear, and our
hearts, so that we might understand,
and our minds, that the wonders
of eternity might be unfolded,
and spread out before us
in a breathtaking
panorama.

The way to
comprehend the hidden
treasures of knowledge that
are scattered as pearls across the
wide expanse of our experience, is
by pressing forward with dedication
to feast upon the words of Christ. As
we do so, we will receive the physical
and spiritual strength and nourishment
that is needed to continue our search.
During that arduous journey by faith
to enlightenment, the Spirit will
support and sustain us with
a revelatory fervor.

The
Atonement
of Jesus Christ
can assure us that we
will be resurrected and will
live forever. But it asks us to
do a bit more. We must organize
ourselves, and "prepare every needful
thing; and establish a house, even a house
of prayer, a house of fasting, a house of faith
a house of learning, a house of glory, (and) a
house of order." (D&C 88:119). In effect, we
must create and maintain a house that has
been dedicated to God, that we might
inherit not only immortality, which
is freely given to all, but also
the greater gift of eternal
life, which is reserved
for those who have
increased in both
wisdom and
stature.

We must not
exhaust our resources
in an attempt to maintain
a vacation retreat in Babylon as
a refuge from life on the strait and
narrow path. Such diversions will cause
us to lose traction, impede our forward
momentum, derail us from our footing
on Gospel sod, and delay our progress
toward our determined destination
that has been envisioned by the
foreknowledge of God.

If we hope to successfully
deal with the inequalities of
life and escape the quicksands
of self-pity, we must personalize
the lessons of the Atonement, and
that is best accomplished during the
hour of prayer that is found within
Sacrament service. As we ponder the
Savior's forgiveness of our sins, we
visualize Him standing before the
golden gate of heaven, patiently
waiting for us to acknowledge
the transcendent beauty of
His power to transform
our lives.

The
celestial compass
of the Spirit is calibrated
to be oriented toward truth,
and to always be available to guide
the faithful to a safe haven. It is also
there for those who have lost their way,
to bring them into the fold of the Good
Shepherd, or to show them how to return
to the security of the community of
Christ from which they may have
strayed in a moment of
weakness.

It is only the witness of the Holy Ghost that can unshackle us from the unpleasant consequences of Justice. Darkness is the conjoined twin of misery, but it is the obedience of faith that frees us to embrace truth, to make intelligent choices, to perform purposefully, to carry on convincingly, and to progress persistently; in short, to rise above the cares of the world through the Atonement of Christ.

Even though
we might currently
be dead weight, thru the
sacrifice of the Savior He will
manifest the strength to carry us
until we have been revitalized, to
walk without becoming weary, and
to run without fainting. But make
no mistake, we will need the light
of the Atonement to disperse the
weight of the darkness that is
always encroaching upon
our world.

We know
that our weaknesses
can damage the fibers that
have been woven by God into
the fabric of our lives. We simply
turn to the inventory of thread that
has been provided by the Holy Ghost,
that enables us to weave new patterns
reflecting our celebration of faith,
and even more importantly, the
strength that is found in its
revelatory expression.

To have the
unlimited freedom
to choose for ourselves
in an atmosphere that is so
full of dangerous deceptions,
enticing entrapments, soothing
seductions, and perilous pathways,
entails great risk. In the Gospel, we
are introduced to a sanctuary that is
remarkably untainted from the blood
and sins of this generation, where we
may flee from Spiritual Babylon, to
faithfully exercise our agency
to be, and to become.

Our faith in
The Plan prompts
us to examine what
it means to be anxiously
engaged, inspires us to plumb
the depths of our commitment to
the Savior, sensitizes us to the nobility
of His work, expands upon our visions of
immortality, personalizes His Atonement,
and stimulates us to remain consciously
aware of the promise of eternal life,
and of our close proximity to
heavenly precincts.

Even as their
ears are assaulted
by sounding brass and
tinkling cymbals, those with
a strong testimony of repentance
will find within the Atonement of
Christ the ability to sift through the
discordant cacophony of confusing
voices to find rhythms of revealed
truth and a harmonious balance
between heaven and earth that
leads to forgiveness of sin.
Our craving to be clean
finds its expression in
celestial sparks that
ignite our desire
to continually
repent.

There has been planted within each of us the key to theology, that we might be able to recognize when The Plan of our God has worked its magic. It is when the Spirit of the Lord falls upon us, and we are filled with joy. When we are clean, we enjoy a peace of conscience that will defy any explanation.

Those who
settle for the moral
mediocrity of character
crippling personality flaws
can never get enough of what
they don't need, because what
they don't need will never
satisfy them. Whether we
know it or not, we live
and move and have
our being because
of the Savior's
Atonement.

We see
God's divine
design each time
we exercise our ability
to look beyond telestial
temptations and temporal
trivia; when we possess the
will to adjust our perspective
so the vision of heaven becomes
a powerful motivator for good,
even as we remain mired in
the telestial winter of the
lone and dreary
world.

We are here
to incorporate into the
conduct of our lives the Haz
Mat Protocol of The Plan, that
will detoxify us from the cares
and conditioning influences
of the world, and from the
homogenization process
that can occur as we
are worn down by
the vicissitudes
of life.

There will always exist among us those stubborn souls who doggedly refuse to repent by confessing their sins to Deity. They persistent in looking to gods of wood and stone that may only temporarily soothe their temporal and spiritual trauma. But, ultimately, we are here to take advantage of Christ's Atonement to redeem us from our self-inflicted misery.

When we
are dealing
with weaknesses
in our contractions
that push forward the
Lord's agenda, relying on
the power of the Atonement
and considering the efficacy
of the Sacrament quickens us
to bear our solemn witness
with a renewed conviction,
without the danger of
becoming zealously
overassertive.

Without
knowledge,
there can be no
faith; without faith,
there can be no light,
and without light there
can be no recognition of
religious truth; and without
spiritual enlightenment, when
one of the three elements of
faith, light, and truth is lost,
then all must be forsaken.
Our fortunes rest upon the
basis of how completely
we embrace this
trifecta.

The temple ordinance directs us to make wardrobe changes out of our soiled clothing into clean garments. It will even require occasional therapy, in the form of a spiritual massage for relief from the bumps and bruises that we'll receive during a journey through mortality that promises to have its fair share of potholes and washouts in the road that we take.

In between
the sights and
sounds, rides and
attractions, and thrills
and spills of our earthly
theme-park experience, the
endowment teaches us how to
use spiritual hygiene practices
to remove the grit and grime
that accumulate as a part of
life, but that always threaten
to foul our inner workings
and curtail our progress
along the pathway that
leads to perfection.

Mortality promises us not just nurturing rain, but also the mud that must inevitably follow. It is our lot in life to dutifully trudge along past potholes and other obstacles on rocky roads that are uphill most of the way and that face an unrelenting headwind. But real disciples would never murmur, nor question God's wisdom. He knows all things, while we see only imperfectly.

Altho our best intentions be noble, vision without work is dreamery, and even if we work, without vision, it is drudgery. If we focus our faith and work with vision, however, if we work in tandem with the Holy Ghost, it will be our good fortune to soar among the eagles in our lives, rather than walk with the turkeys who only scratch out a meager existence along the way, subsiding on grubs and worms.

We embrace
the temple because
it is there that we receive
a transfusion of the spiritual
element. It is a heavenly dialysis
center, where worldly contaminants
may be removed from our spirits,
because we are simply incapable
of accomplishing the task on
our own. The resources we
need are found nowhere
but in the Atonement
of Jesus Christ.

Our baptism
for the remission
of our sins activates
the redemption exemption
that is a codicil to the Law
of Justice. The terms of our
lease on life are renegotiated
by the Savior to our everlasting
advantage. All is accomplished
solely on the strength of His
infinite and eternal
Atonement.

Our engagement with life in a forum of free will propels us onward toward immortality and eternity, as long as we are obedient to our covenants and we rely upon the Atonement of Christ. These are the protocols that will keep the sand of sin out of the gears of the machine that was created in heaven for the benefit of gods in embryo.

People think
that they can be happy
if they wander and play,
forgetting that a key feature
of God's Plan, the purpose of
our existence, is to ponder and
pray. This leads us to appreciate
the Atonement, and to speedily
repent of our sins. Only then,
will we find the happiness
that has been prepared
for the Saints.

When we are
completely engaged
in The Plan of Salvation,
it is our regularly recurring
repentance that will bless us with
repetitive moments of confirmation;
when we will declare, as did those in
Zarahemla, that through the miracle
of forgiveness, by the power of the
Atonement, our hearts have once
again been changed through
faith on the name of
Jesus Christ.

Those who undertake to
grapple with the permutations
and combinations of mortality
realize that the key of knowledge
may be employed by both those who
are in poverty and those who abound
in wealth. It is engaged by both fame
and obscurity, exercised in sickness and
in health, put to good use by those with
influence as well as by those who are
living in anonymity, and it may be
successfully retained by beauty
and the beast. God is no
respecter of persons.

Revelation from God
sets us free to be creative,
and our creativity sets us free to
properly plan before we come face to
face with the crises of life. It prevents
our poor performance and it mitigates
consequences. As we learn to rely upon
the doctrine of Christ that is taught by
the Spirit, we internalize its elements.
This allows us to surrender ourselves
to its infinite possibilities, without
reservation. Therein, we find our
individuality and avenues for
personal expression, and in
the end, we discover our
freedom to "become."

The priesthood
energizes the grace
of God by administering
the ordinances of salvation,
sanctification, justification, and
exaltation, that allow us to receive
the blessings of the Gospel by binding
us to Him through covenants of action.
The temple endowment, in particular,
helps us to enjoy a larger perspective
of our place in the cosmos, as well
as a greater understanding of
The Plan of Salvation and
of our divine potential.

The faithful quickly learn that darkness cannot be carried into a lighted room. They seize every occasion to be enveloped within the brilliance of The Plan. They have determined to face toward the Son, so the shadows will always be behind them. Darkness will still exist, but its companions that take the form of apprehension, trepidation, uncertainty, and fear will be out of sight and out of mind.

As
we look
around at a
world that seems
to have gone mad,
the temple stands as
a light that has been set
on a hill; an island in the
storm providing refuge from
the uncertainties and vagaries
of life. It speaks a language
of stability, direction, and
purpose to those who are
afraid, uncertain, and
hesitant in their
faith.

The temple stands as a solemn witness of just how we will behave if we are left to our own devices, after having received instruction regarding what we should do. The Savior is the Architect of the Cosmos, and we lend our support to His pillars of creation when we raise our right arms to the square.

It is in the
temple that we
get our bearings
on eternity, and we
take a fix on the stars
in the heavens. It is there
that our telestial tendencies
are transformed into celestial
sureties. This process is not one
of maturation, but of generation,
as we are "born again" in that
divine delivery room whose
name is The House of
the Lord.

When we
invite the Holy
Ghost to be Guru,
Guide, and Governor,
we don't allow ourselves
to get in the thick of thin
things. Instead, we establish
an equilibrium that is centered
far from the madding crowd, at a
safe distance from the ego-filled
minds of mediocre men. We are
insulated from the clamor, the
confusion, and the cares of
the world, and enjoy a
firmness that is
unshakable.

Our
Father has
implanted in our
beating hearts the
steady rhythm of hope
that we will continue to
be able to utilize the tools
that He has provided to make
the vital distinction between
knowledge and wisdom, and
to use them to make correct
choices that are based upon
the intelligent application
of the former in order to
capture the blessings
of the latter.

Sooner or later, there will be for each of us who has undergone a spiritual heart transplant a moment in the sun, when the steady light of understanding illuminates our minds so that the divine potential of the new organs audibly beating in our chests might be confirmed by a deep and abiding faith in the Savior's Atonement.

The white-hot sparks of faith that have been struck off the divine anvil of God may smolder for a while, before they ignite the flame of our resolve. But when they do, we will have developed the power to do whatsoever thing is right, and that is to throw ourselves on the mercy seat of our Lord and Savior, and to rely upon His Atonement to save us from our sins.

The
Atonement
allows us to see
beyond the limited
horizon of our sight;
to be touched by a vision
of the virtue of the word of
God. Our faith enables us to
savor revealed truth with a
discriminating taste that
discerns the distinctive
flavor of eternal
worlds.

The
Atonement
draws upon the
magnificent power
of all three members
of the Godhead, so that
we may become increasingly
receptive to flashes of insight;
to be cast off into streams of
revelation that carry us along
in the quickening currents of
direct experience with our
Heavenly Father, with
Jesus Christ, and
with the Holy
Ghost.

The Atonement of Christ encourages an interrelationship between our physical and spiritual well-being and obedience, that must exist if we hope to nurture faith to recognize a divine design during the assembly of our mortal tabernacles that were created by God and were destined by Him to be transformed into the holy tabernacles of our spirits.

Faith is more than our intellectual assent. Its influence extends as far as our deeds. Therefore, works that reflect our reliance upon the Atonement of our Savior Jesus Christ become an important companion to our faith.

Our testimony of truth, and in particular of the Atonement, includes these three essential elements. Initially, is our introduction to an eternal principle. Second, is our correct understanding of the Lord's counsel concerning the principle, and finally, is our experience with the principle, which is the fruits of faith. (See Galatians 5:2).

When
situational
ethics guide our
behavior, and when
every man walketh in
his own way, and after
the image of his own god,
the erosion of faith, followed
by the chaotic crash of cultural
cohesion and stability, is inevitable.
Neither tinkling cymbals nor sounding
brass holds a candle to the light that
is shed by The Plan of Salvation on
the questions of where we came
from, why we are here, and
where we are going.

When we
are touched
by a revelatory,
spirit, we accept the
challenge extended by
the temple endowment
to expand our horizons.
We determine to wrap our
thoughts around the unknown
possibilities of existence. Then,
when we receive the anointing
of the Holy Ghost, we will not
be able to rest "until the last
enemy has been conquered,
and death is destroyed."
Ultimately, truth will
reign triumphant."
(Parley P. Pratt).

The
Holy Ghost
puts the day to
day elements of The
Plan in perspective, that
we might more clearly be
able to distinguish the grey
-toned obstacles that lie in
our path. These barriers to our
progression will then stand out
in sharp contrast against the
polychromatic backdrop of
the design that God has
created for each
one of us.

Our faith pushes
us toward perfection,
which often means that we
will persevere until we feel
that we have no more to give.
It is at the point of exhaustion
that we cast our burdens on a
power that is greater than
ourselves. It is in our
Savior that we hope
to survive the
ordeal.

Faith is impotent when it does not lead to purposeful performance. It is the sizzle without the steak. Real faith involves a vital, personal self-commitment to a practical belief. But in the end, even our belief will ring hollow if it lacks the confirming witness of the Holy Ghost, Who is the companion of faith.

We are here at
this time and at this
place to be born again by
the power of the Atonement
of Jesus Christ, Who orients us
toward the expansive laws of
hidden worlds rather than to
the restrictive parameters of
temporal surroundings. The
miracle, however, is that
our nurturing must be
accompanied by the
refining process
of repentance.

We are imperfect mortals who are struggling to believe what we do not see. The reward of maturing faith is to see what we believe. Some things just have to be believed to be seen, and so, it is faith in the Savior that initializes the obedience of faith, to know by the witness of the Holy Ghost.

We
are here to
repent, for that is
just the prescription
the Doctor ordered to
treat the religious fever
that elevates our testimony
temperature enough to get
our juices flowing with a
visceral appreciation of
the sacrifice of the
Savior thru His
Atonement.

We are here on
this orb to redefine
and redesign what had
heretofore been stumbling
blocks. They are repurposed
into the very stepping-stones
that are needed to conquer
our doubts, strengthen our
confidence, and surmount
the obstacles we will all
encounter along the
pathways of our
progression.

Woven within
the material that
makes up the tapestry
of mortal life, there are
sometimes "dark threads
that are as needful in the
Weaver's skillful hand as
the threads of gold and
silver, in the pattern
He has planned."
(B. Franklin).

We
who have
the faith to
be born again
are set free by the
Atonement of Christ
to reach our potential.
We are as the acorns of
mighty oaks, vitalized by
faith and basking in the
nurturing influence of
God to grow to the
full stature of
our spirits.

When we end our mortal journey, we will remember the celestial signposts that took us past the conceptual cul-de-sacs, the doctrinal dead ends, and the telestial traffic that always threatened to detour us from the strait and narrow way. We will be forever grateful for the ordinances that exposed us to direct experience with the perfect law of liberty, and that permitted us to exchange the uncertain course that had been adopted by those bound for the telestial kingdom, for the reality of celestial certainty. We will understand that an uncommitted recognition of Jesus Christ doesn't promise an inheritance in the Celestial Kingdom, because Christians of convenience don't have the fire that is ignited by covenants. Many honorable people who accept the Savior will still inherit the Terrestrial Kingdom. According to the scriptures, they did not receive the Gospel, the testimony of Jesus, the prophets, or the covenants. Thus, they "will not be gathered with the Saints, to be caught up unto the Church of the Firstborn, and received into the cloud." (D&C 76:102).

When this
life is over, some of us
are going to hell. But that
is not necessarily a bad thing. Hell
is a reformatory that has been designed
to improve the quality of our moral nature.
It is a penitentiary where faith can still convict
us of our sins. It was designed to help disobedient
spirits to recognize that Jesus Christ is the Mediator
of the Covenant thru His Atonement. D&C 76 teaches
that the Gospel is taught to the spirits kept in that
prison. If, while there, they exercise their agency
and accept not only Christ, but also the fulness
of His Gospel, is it not reasonable that they
might also inherit celestial glory with the
Saints? Surely, this is why we build
temples and, without prejudice,
perform vicarious work for
all of our kindred
dead.

Temple marriage and our eternal progress involve making covenants with the Lord. Promised blessings include being together "in time, and through all eternity" (D&C 132:19), being exalted in the glory of the Celestial Kingdom with Heavenly Father and Jesus Christ (D&C 131:1-3, & 132:23), while inheriting "thrones, kingdoms, principalities, powers (and) dominions" (D&C 132:19), having children in the eternities (D&C 1321:19, & 30-31), enjoying divine attributes, (and) becoming as 'gods,' because we have been given all power.
(D&C 1322:20-21).

In 1995, the First Presidency of the Church, together with the Quorum of the Twelve Apostles, prophetically issued The Proclamation on The Family, because it is the basic building block of eternity. It is the best defense against an indifferent world, and the best institution of higher education. It is certified by our Heavenly Father, and has received His divine approbation. The creation of the eternal family is the end product of the ordinances of the temple that link us to our forefathers and to our descendants in an unbroken chain that binds the telestial to the celestial, the earth to the heavens, and the temporal world to eternity.

Heavenly Father's children, who have grown to appreciate His spiritual stature, will use the 'Atonement' password to get by Security at the portal of heaven. As they approach His throne, they will look back and witness the transcendent beauty of the gate through which they, as heirs of the kingdom, have entered, which will be "like unto circling flames of fire; Also the blazing throne of God, wherein" there shall be "seated the Father and the Son." And the "beautiful streets of that kingdom," shall have "the appearance of being paved with gold." (D&C 137:2-4). Thus, is described in beautiful imagery, the power of our covenants that are only made possible through the Atonement of Christ.

Maybe
The Plan
will leave God's
disobedient children
in the Spirit Prison of The
Unjust only long enough for
them to recognize the error of
their ways, and to motivate them
to make behavioral changes that are
balanced with the teachings, ordinances,
and covenants of the Gospel. Recognizing
their transgressions, such individuals might
be required to pay directly for the sins they
had committed in mortality that had fallen
outside the merciful sphere of influence of
the Atonement. Such punishment would be
eternally and endlessly in harmony with
the Law of Mercy, and it would seem to
also satisfy the demands of Justice,
allowing God' perfect Plan to
move forward, in harmony
with His bold mission
statement.

All of
us will be
tested by trials
and temptations,
and we will make
mistakes. But we will
rise above our failures
because of our love of the
Savior and His Atonement. It
is in the next act that all the
mysteries will be solved, all the
pieces of the puzzle will be put in
their proper place, all the confusion
that had aforetime tormented us will
be put to rest, and everything will be
made right. For that to happen, we
need to be up and about, starting
right now, by making our way
past every obstacle on the
path that leads to the
feet of the Savior.

Those familiar
with the scripting of
the Three Act Play might
be aware of the Master's well
known reputation for theatrical
encore. Denigrators might see only
a frivolous repetition, or even look
in vain for even a brief intermission
from the holy Gospel's active and vital
engagement with life. However, sooner or
later, Heavenly Father will surely extend
an invitation to each of the participants
in the Play to have their moment in the
sun. Their minds will be illuminated by
the Light of Christ or the Holy Ghost.
In a spiritual awakening, they will
experience a confirmation of the
divine potential that had always
rested within their souls, but
may have lain dormant
while waiting for its
quickening by the
Spirit.

To those who prepare themselves thru temple attendance, the Lord "will shew wonders in the heavens and in the earth, (with) blood, and fire and pillars of smoke." (Joel 2:30). When He revealed Himself to Isaiah, his appearance was so commanding that "the posts of the doors moved at the voice of him that cried, and the house was filled with smoke. Then, (said Isaiah), Woe is me! For I am undone." (Isaiah 6:4-5). His physical frame could barely tolerate the Presence of God. He would need health in his navel and marrow in his bones, as well as strength in his loins and in his sinews, if he ever hoped to be successfully admitted into the great and terrible presence of the Lord Himself. (See D&C 89:18, Proverbs 3:8, & Job 40:16).

As we
think of our
journey to the veil,
we recall the wisdom
of Sir Winston Churchill:
"There comes for each of us
an extraordinary moment when
we are figuratively tapped on the
shoulder and offered a chance to do
a very special thing, unique to ourselves
and fitted to our talents. What a tragedy
if that moment should find us unprepared
or unqualified for that which would be our
finest hour." Each time we stand before God,
angels, and witnesses at the veil of the temple,
it is a fitting conclusion to our finest hour
that was spent as an eager participant in
the ordinance of the endowment.

Since there
is opposition in
all things, even as there
is faith, so must there also
be its worldly counterpart. In
our day, the grip of fear paralyzes
many of God's children. Today, more
than ever, we need the Holy Ghost. We
need the assurance of peace, that our
lives are moving in the direction of
our dreams, and that it is thru the
Atonement that we are given the
tools we will need to hitch our
wagons to the stars that have
been fortuitously positioned
by God to guide us back
to our heavenly home.

Over time, our mystical relationship with God becomes indelibly etched into our spiritual identity. We become perfect in our faith to make a connection with Deity. That is how members of The Church of Jesus Christ of Latter-day Saints presume to declare that it is our destiny to rule as kings and queens, priests and priestesses, in the house of Israel, to rule over kingdoms, thrones, principalities, powers, dominions, and exaltations. The apple does not fall very far from the tree. Our identities, and that of God, will have become indistinguishable from each other. That can only happen if we receive both His image and likeness in our countenances, in the process of a mind-expanding spiritual metamorphosis that we can, for now, only reference with fear and trembling before the Lord.

Marriage that is ordained
of God is the noblest expression
of the relationship between a man
and a woman. If a couple considers it a
covenant representing the divine model, it
is more likely that they will start off on the
right footing, as they work toward their shared
potential. In fact, matrimony is one of the seven
sacraments of the Catholic Church. This is a point
upon which its members are in agreement with their
Latter-day Saint neighbors. We all believe that the
sacraments introduce us to God's grace, and that
in a coming day, we will be invited to return to
His presence. Intuitively, we all believe that
we will be together with our loved ones
in eternity, in family relationships
that are founded upon marriage
that is ordained of God.

As we wend
our way through life, past
great and spacious buildings,
we are only able to enjoy a godly
walk and conversation because of the
Atonement, which can save us from our
natural state of carnality, sensuality, and
devilish inclinations. It activates the Law of
Mercy, which mitigates for those who conform
to its requirements the effects of the first Law,
that demands Justice. It lifts us to a state of
holiness, spirituality, angelic innocence, and
happiness. It prepares us to feel comfortable
in our heavenly home, where we will find
that we are in the pleasant company of
legions of angels who will serenade
us with lullabies that express love
for us in the rapturous language
of the Celestial Kingdom.

The day is not far off when our mortal bodies must put on immortality. This may be accomplished as we are carried as upon the wings of eagles, or angelic hosts, into the greater light of heaven. Just as ultraviolet light is used in sterilization, (ultraviolet germicidal irradiation – UVGI), could it be that it is the physical phenomenon of God's unearthly aura that purifies and renews our battle-weary and sin-stained souls? Though our "sins be as scarlet, they shall be as white as snow; though they be red like crimson, they shall be as wool." (Isaiah 1:18).

Those poor
sin-bound souls
who, through no fault of
their own, have been denied the
chance in this life to embrace the
Gospel, will be judged according to
their more limited understanding of the
doctrines and principles that are related
to deliverance. Therefore, when they stand
before the Judgment Bar, they will vary in
their accountability to law. The reach of
the Atonement lies in its ability to bless
our lives, without regard to individual
circumstances. It is both infinite and
eternal in its scope, because each
of us must play the hand we
have been dealt. The Lord,
however, has resources
that are sufficient
to cover all of
our bets.

After the dust has settled, and our favorite Church leader has been quoted, and when all of the relevant scriptures have been cited, the fact remains that we have not received the revelations that answer the questions that relate to our progression between kingdoms of glory. But intuitively, we desperately want to believe that it must be possible. When, as patrons, we attend the temple and perform vicarious work for the dead, we do not consider the conduct of their lives. When the veil seems almost transparent, and we sense inaudible whispering from the other side, the Holy Ghost speaks to our souls in a language of peace regarding the absolute perfection of God's Plan of Happiness.

The verbal exchange that takes place at the veil is a rehearsal. It prepares us to be clothed with both immortality and eternal life; to more closely resemble our Father in Heaven in His image and in His likeness. The dialogue that takes place in the endowment suggests that we are gods and goddesses in embryo, and that our genome is divine. It extends the promise that it is our destiny to mature until, in an eternal progression that relies upon the infinite and eternal Atonement of Christ, we have been prepared to go where no-one has ever gone before and to loose the latchets of our shoes in the sanctity of space, before we dare to walk in the footsteps of God.

The reach of the Atonement of Christ extends so far that it has power to neutralize the sins of the best of us and the worst of us, and those of everyone else whose transgressions lie in between; not only of the living, but also the of the dead. Of its temporal and eternal influence, there are no limits. It waits upon our initiative to manifest its energy through the vicarious work of our Lord and Savior, as well as through our own vicarious efforts that are performed in the temple. We are transported along with our kindred dead into a harmony with heaven, into the presence of God.

Each of us
pays dearly for
our secular education,
and we expect a return on
our investment. Our introduction
to Gospel instruction is equivalent
to engaging in an independent study
fine arts program. Its requirements for
admission are simply a ready heart and
a willing mind, and there is no temporal
tuition. Its design and its purpose is to
teach us what we need to know and
do, that God may guide us back to
His heavenly home, to live and
love with Him in His kingdom.
He will always leave the
porch light burning
for us.

In an episode of "Star Trek", Q told Captain Picard: "You just don't get it, do you Jean Luc? The trial never ends. We wanted to see if you had the ability to expand your mind and your horizons. And for one brief moment you did. For that one fraction of a second, you were open to options that you had never considered. That is the exploration that awaits you. It is not mapping stars and studying nebula, but instead charting the unknown possibilities of existence." We don't have to book passage on Galaxy Class Starships to do that. We just need to make time to frequent the celestial observatory of the House of The Lord, to explore the far reaches of eternity.

We are baptized
that those who have
died without having had
the opportunity to hear about
The Plan of Salvation might also
partake of eternal life. The Atonement
is the gold standard not only for those who
are the living, but also of vicarious work for
the dead. In our day, the Savior has delegated
authority to the members of His Church to follow
His example, to act in behalf of the dead; of those
who are unable to perform saving ordinances for
themselves, since they have passed beyond the
veil and are living without tangible bodies
in the Spirit World, while they await their
own spiritual renewal, redemption,
and resurrection.

The temple stands as a bastion of spiritual security, and obedience to the commandments is the only requirement for entry. If we seek "all the days of (our) lives for that which (we) cannot obtain, and ... have sought for happiness in doing iniquity, which thing is contrary to the nature of that righteousness which is in our great and Eternal Head," we cannot go there and we must face the consequences of our actions. (Helaman 13:38). It will be then, under the most difficult of circumstances, that the uttermost farthing must be paid, that the demands of Justice might be satisfied after the required reform has finally take place.

Those who listen carefully to the words of the temple endowment will exercise the authority vested in them to claim their birthright, and to harness the power of the priesthood, "to break mountains, to divide the seas, to dry up waters, to turn them out of their course; to put at defiance the armies of nations, to divide the earth, to break every band, to stand in the presence of God ... to do all things according to his command (to) subdue principalities and powers, and this by the will of the Son of God which was from before the foundation of the world. And (those with) this faith, coming up unto this order of God, (will be) translated and taken up into heaven." (J.S.T. Genesis 14:30-32).

Obedience to
temple covenants
gives us the chance to
catch a glimpse of heaven.
"Abundance is multiplied unto
(us) through the manifestations of
the Spirit" that are so profoundly felt
that they seem to overflow, as we realize
our righteous objectives. (D&C 70:13). These
stay in focus because the temple's spiritual
guideposts provide us with an orientation
that is centered on eternity. They bless
us with the only proven perspective in
a world that is overflowing with
myriad voices that are in a
fierce competition for
our attention.

The
Mountain of
the Lord's House, as
it has been described in
scripture, is an allegorical
and figurative representation
of the refuge of Zion in the Last
Days, when it "shall be established in
the tops of the mountains." (2 Nephi 12:2).
Whether it is a high place where God dwells,
a habitation of revelation, or perhaps the temple
itself, Latter-day Saints have sometimes restricted
the application of this phrase to one area, that
of the intermountain west, specifically to the
Valley of the Great Salt Lake. However, this
interpretation may be too narrow. All who
have been to the temple believe it to be
the invisible summit of imagination,
where cool air exists, and where
the one true God lives in
His celestial glory.

As we
begin to embrace
the creative expression
of the endowment, we realize
that it is its energy and its vitality
that helps us to appreciate God. We begin
to feel the divine potential within us. We feel
the confidence to ask seemingly simple questions
that can have profound answers and implications
that shake our world, spreading like the ripples
radiating outward from a rock thrown into the
still waters of the pond of our imaginations.
Our temple reflections reveal a revelatory
machine for the making of Gods, and
we visualize ourselves intimately
interconnected with the
process.

We undertake a journey of faith when we go to the House of The Lord, that, in covenants of exaltation, we might accept our Father's Firstborn Son and His Gospel. If we do so, we thereby avoid the weeping and wailing and gnashing of teeth that would otherwise accompany our recognition that the days of our probation were past because we had procrastinated the day of our salvation until it was everlastingly too late, and our destruction had been made sure. (See Helaman 13:38).

The Atonement of Christ blesses us to be repetitively revitalized. It re-introduces us to a magical kingdom where our hopes and dreams really will come true, and we will live happily ever after. When we wish upon the Star of David, it will make no difference who we are. Anything that our hearts have desired will come to us, because our Heavenly Father will have put the energy of our souls into our prayers. No request we make to Him will be too extreme, for we will dwell in righteousness.

It is only
our profound obedience
and recurring repentance that
release us from the bondage of
sin and qualify us by worthiness to
enjoy the blessings of the temple. The
Atonement of Jesus Christ, which is the
centerpiece of the instruction that we
receive in the endowment, allows us
to overcome our limitations while
unleashing the powers of heaven.
It shatters the glass ceiling of
death by breaking its bands
for all who have ever
lived on the earth,
and for all who
ever will.

In the Spirit World, those who accept the Fulness of the Gospel and have had the necessary ordinances of exaltation performed in their behalf in the temple will be heirs of the Celestial Kingdom of glory. "These shall dwell in the presence of God and his Christ forever and ever." (D&C 76:62). When the gates of hell swing wide open for the repentant faithful of every generation, we will have witnessed an example of the Atonement of Jesus Christ at its best. For both the living and dead, "the presence of the Lord shall be as the melting fire that burneth, and as the fire which causeth the waters to boil." (D&C 133:41).

When
we have
been born
again thru the
Sacrament, our
orientation is more
toward the expansive
laws of the eternal world
than it is to the restrictive
confines that are defined by
our physical surroundings. The
Spirit guides us to the physicality
of heartfelt repentance, and to an
appreciation of the otherworldly
doctrine of the Atonement. The
Plan of God bridges both time
and space, by guiding us to
a condition that is more
one of "becoming" than
it is of simply
"being."

As we draw near to the veil of the temple, we are reminded of the experience of the people of Zarahemla after the crucifixion of the Lord. From the unseen world, "there was a voice heard among all the inhabitants of the earth, upon all the face" of the land. (3 Nephi 9:1). It was not a deafening voice of a hundred decibels, but simply a quiet sound that was heard by everyone regardless of their temporal surroundings. It was a voice quite unlike any sound that had ever before been heard, for it came from immortal lips with a profound effect on both the heavens and the earth.

Heavenly Father
wants us to burst beyond
our self-imposed limitations.
That is why He has ordained a Plan
where we may one day attain His stature
and become all that He now is. But we may
do this only if we incorporate into our
own being and nature His image and
likeness. Thru that process, He has
ordained that our corruptible
bodies will become clean,
pure, and overflowing
with light.

Our endowment in the temple relates to our physical and spiritual nature, and dictates that we will inherit our bodies in the resurrection and be reacquainted with our spirits, never again to be separated. Our spirits and our bodies shall be reunited in their perfect form; both our limbs and our joints shall be restored to their proper frame. (See Alma 11:43). In the interim, our bodies must be kept as pure and as holy as are our spirits, in order for the covenants of the temple to bless our lives as envisioned by our Father.

Because of the veil, we can only indirectly appreciate the eternities. As we seek learning in the House of the Lord, even by study and also by faith, "we can make our lives sublime, and departing, leave behind us footprints on the sands of time." (Longfellow). But if those footprints do not lead to the temple, they may be washed away by the wave action of the world that incessantly beats upon the shores of our spiritual integrity. It is our Fathers hope that we take advantage of the tide in our affairs, which, taken at the flood, will lead on to fortune in the glory of His Celestial Kingdom. (See Shakespeare, "Julius Caesar").

When we stand before
the veil in the temple, we
come face to face with eternity.
Mortality itself loses significance.
We appreciate how 'See you later' might
no longer be part of our vocabulary. As
we pass through the veil into the presence
of the Lord, we no longer view time as a
predator that stalked us all of our lives.
We now see it as a traveling companion
that accompanied us on our journey
through mortality, reminding us to
cherish the experiences that have
led us to this special 'moment'
that spans all eternity.

Those who
were denied the
chance in this life to
embrace the Gospel will be
judged according to their more
limited understanding of the doctrines
and principles of God's Plan. Therefore,
when they approach the Bar of Justice, they
will necessarily vary in their accountability
to law. Therein lies the hidden power of the
Holy Ghost to ultimately bless their lives.
Beside the Savior, He will become their
advocate, and He will justify them
as long as their behavior had
been in harmony with the
illumination they had
received from the
Light of Christ.

In the not too
distant future, there
will come for each of us
a day in the sun. It will be
a great and dreadful day when
we will be asked to stand and give
our sworn deposition before God and
angels, who will depose the witness of
the Holy Ghost. On the issue of faith,
depending upon our answer, we will
be counted among the sheep or the
goats, and find ourselves on the
right hand of God, or on His
left hand. It all depends
on us, and on how we
have conducted
our lives.

Possibly reflecting
upon his temple experiences,
and recognizing the power of its
ordinances, Parley P. Pratt exclaimed:
"I have received the holy anointing, and I
can never rest until the last enemy has been
conquered, death destroyed, and truth reigns
triumphant." His joy was full, because he had
complete confidence in the capacity of
The Great Plan of Mercy to redeem
him from his sins, and to propel
him in the direction of his
celestial destiny.

It is within
the walls of the
temple that we begin in
earnest our preparation for
immortality. It is there that our
eyes are really opened, our vision
is perfected, and we are taught how
to raise our sight so that it rests above
the artificial horizon of mortality. It is
there, in the House of The Lord, that we
take a long look at the wonders of
eternity, and discover that our
future lies, not on the earth,
but in heaven.

Our finest hours are when our unexpected challenges are met with extraordinary efforts. Just like the Seven Dwarfs, when we embrace the tenets of the Gospel, we whistle while we work out our salvation, because of the miracle of the Atonement. We learn how our Heavenly Father has linked our own efforts to those of His Son. Happiness, as it turns out, is the object and design of our existence, and it will be the end thereof, if we follow the path of repentance that leads to it.

Nothing that takes place in the temple is of direct benefit to the patrons who have already received their endowment and participated in the other ordinances of exaltation. Their service is wholly, completely, and unequivocally in behalf of those who have passed beyond the veil, and it is through their efforts that those who might have otherwise been forgotten are clothed in the robes of the holy priesthood and blessed with an endowment of power, that they might pass by angels and witnesses, to enter the presence of the Lord.

Our forever families
that have been sealed in the
temple provide the mortar that
holds the parapets of the Celestial
Kingdom together. Family grounds us
to mortality, but also anchors us to the
Infinite, by blessing us with a perspective
that is eternal. Families that are bound
together by covenants made with God
provide a much needed longitudinal
perspective in those societies where
just about everything, including
relationships, is increasingly
disposable. When there has
been no deposit made,
how there can be an
expectation of
a return?

Profound obedience
and recurring repentance
release us from the bondage of
sin, and qualify us by worthiness to
enjoy the blessings of the temple. The
Atonement of Jesus Christ, which is the
centerpiece of the instruction that we
receive in the endowment, allows us
to overcome our limitations while
unleashing the powers of heaven
in our behalf. It shatters the
bands of death, and throws
open the gates of the
Celestial Kingdom
itself.

When we stand before
the Bar of Justice, we will
acknowledge that the covenants
we had made in the temple were not
haphazard or arbitrary, with corollaries,
footnotes, addenda, and exceptions to the
rule. Our obedience required neither analysis
nor interpretation by legal counsel, and our
accounting demanded no interpretation by
an expensive C.P.A. The endowment has
been clearly established and carefully
clarified with purposeful precision so
that there can be no disputation
concerning its validity or its
accessibility. It is striking
in its simplicity.

In a coming day, when we
face eternity, as we surely must,
the spiritual element in which we are
then immersed will transform our mortal
clay. Until that time comes, while we yet tarry
on the earth, we might ask ourselves under what
circumstances does that element quicken us now,
and how can the pure knowledge that flows out
of it be vitalized? Surely, it is wisdom that
will make our faces shine, as we embrace
the principles of the endowment.
(See Ecclesiastes 8:1).

The dead are very likely just as concerned about our welfare, as we are about theirs. They may view family history research as a mutually shared avenue of protection from the deceits of the adversary, as an opportunity to receive the assistance we need in the conduct of our lives, and as an inspired program to deepen conversion and bring our eternal families closer together, as light and knowledge are received through the Holy Ghost on both sides of the veil.

Without the
eternal perspective
provided by the endowment,
we are much more likely to define
ourselves only in the present tense. Then,
we will be less inclined to make the kinds
of decisions that reflect our noble lineage,
or to independently develop the attitudes
and habit patterns that will bring us into
conformity with heaven. Our ability to
'be' may be secure, but our ability
to 'become' might never
receive the nurture
it deserves.

When Elijah spoke with the Lord, his experience was so overwhelming that "a great and strong wind rent the mountains, and brake in pieces the rocks before the Lord ... and after the wind (there was) an earthquake ... and after the earthquake a fire." (1 Kings 19:11-12). The Lord's Presence was manifest in representations of the most dramatic forces in nature. At His Second Coming, the Mount of Olives will be rent in twain, and later the whole earth will come together into one land mass as it was in the days before Peleg. (See Genesis 10:25).

The vast and expansive
influence of the Holy Ghost
has the capacity to become the
underlying element of a tapestry
whose design will be revealed, in
all its glory, as an expression of
our being when we attain the full
stature of our spirits. When our
nature finally corresponds to
the harmony of heaven, our
perfect frames will burst
free of the shackles of
our mortal clay, as
vibrant coats of
many colors.

Sooner or later,
when we have attended the
temple frequently enough that
our lives have begun to conform to
the character of God, we will enjoy that
realm of spirit as our natural environment
and we will understand that it is more vibrantly
real than anything we have ever known. In the
meantime, we must beware, lest we strangle
ourselves with illusions of reality, and
with things whose opacity obstructs
our ability to see what is
really there.

The infinite
and eternal Atonement
of our Savior Jesus Christ
is the codicil to the best fire
insurance policy that could ever
have been written, indemnifying us
against the possibility of being burned
as stubble at the last day. As long as
we paid our premiums, we will avoid
being consumed, and we will receive
our immortal bodies as benefits of
the resurrection, to dwell forever
unhurt amid celestial burnings.
Such is the awesome power of
The Great and Eternal Plan
of Deliverance From
Death.

In the temple, when we stand before the veil, we institutionally validate the reality of higher spatial and temporal dimensions in an unseen world. The Pearl of Great Price reinforces the teachings of the endowment, confirming that from their superior vantage point in time, it was the Gods Who organized both the heavens and the earth, and Who divided the light from the darkness, created the waters and the earth, and placed all manner of vegetation thereon. Finally, they watched over those things they had created, and saw that they obeyed.
(See Abraham 4:1-18).

The influence of the Light of Christ encourages us to set our sights upon the pole-star of the Atonement, that was designed by God to point us to the higher plateau of eternal life in the kingdom of heaven. In the meantime, participants in the Three Act Play are independent in the stage of development to which their decisions have led them. We are poised at the edge of forever, and though we may have parked ourselves on complacency plateaus, we need little incentive to consider the unknown possibilities of existence.

Those who have
taken the time to appreciate the
power of the ordinances of the Gospel
are able to visualize the Celestial Kingdom.
They use the Atonement of Christ to move in
its direction. They follow the admonition of the
Savior: "Seek ye first the kingdom of God, and
his righteousness; and all these things shall be
added unto you." (Matthew 6:33). It is through
our participation in these ordinances that we
witness our willingness to be yoked to the
Savior, and that we have taken our Father
in Heaven at His word when He declared
that it is His work and glory to bring
to pass both our immortality and
our eternal life.

Our journey to the veil helps us to realize that when we kill time, we damage our eternal selves, for as the Lord warned, "in an hour when ye think not, the summer shall be past, and the harvest ended, and your souls not saved." (D&C 45:2). We realize that every second of every day, we are one tick of the clock closer to an undiscovered country from whose precincts no traveler will return. A tagline for a popular motel chain reassures us that they'll leave the light on for us. God goes one step better than that promise. He has created a celestial homing beacon whose illumination is a constant reminder that the reward for our struggles will be worth the wrestle.

Brigham Young declared: "How many kingdoms of glory there are, I know not; and how many degrees of glory there are in these kingdoms, I know not; but there are multitudes of them. The kingdoms that God has prepared are innumerable." It is our awakening comprehension that is as a repetitive prelude to our introduction to the glory and wonders of eternity. We aim high, and when we discard the poor lenses of the body, with their myopic view of life, we will look instead upon the rolling vistas of eternity.

The guidance provided by the Holy Ghost makes it possible for us to negotiate the strait and narrow path all the way to the Tree of Life, there to partake of its fruit, which represents eternal life. As we do so, because of the ever present threat of behavioral instability, God has provided us with the covenants that we make in the temple. Therein lies the power of the endowment to reorient us to righteousness, and to recalibrate our moral compass so that it might safely guide us home to the happiness that has been prepared for the Saints.

Frequent temple worship helps us to break away from limiting beliefs. As we brush up against the stars, we are awakened to a new vision that is, at first, blinding, but as our eyes adjust to the light, we might be surprised to see, not only the world as it really is, but also the future as it can be, for us and for our families. Ordinances can impart dignity, nobility, and value to those of our Father's children who have gone on before. They insure that their memory will never be trivialized, and that none of them, in all eternity, will ever be overlooked or forgotten.

In the temple, our souls are freed to go forth from their dwelling places, to discard the poor lenses of our bodies, and peer through the telescope of truth into the infinite reaches of immortality. It is during our journey to the veil that we begin to really appreciate the strength of our position, that we might one day "flourish in immortal youth, unhurt amidst the war of elements, the wreck of matter, and the crash of worlds." (Joseph Addison).

There are some who
may ask themselves: "What
do I want out of life?" but those
with faith in the Atonement instead
wonder to themselves: "What would my
Savior have me do, and have me become?"
With silent lifting minds and with quiet
words softly spoken, we draw near to
the untrespassed sanctity of heaven,
and we put out our hands, that we
might touch, as it were, the face
of God, and live.

When we
pass thru the veil to
enter the Celestial Room
in the House of The Lord, we
realize that we had heretofore
been living in one dimly lighted
corner of reality, and that our very
narrow perspective had somehow been
frozen in time. We will find that we
have returned home, to a far more
comfortable and expansive domain
where both power and authority
take on new meanings that,
aforetime, had been only
dimly perceived.

We are
going to heaven, and
we follow a pulsing stream
of inspiration whose flow has no
temporal boundary and is without
spatial limitation. Thru the Atonement,
we are at one with the mind of God. The
Spirit opens the eyes of our understanding
until we comprehend undreamed of vistas
of otherwise inaccessible experience. Our
heart strings resonate as we consider
the promised blessing of old, that
it is "by the power of the Holy
Ghost that (we) may know
the truth of all things."
(Moroni 10:5).

The temple
prepares us for
the realization that
our mortal experience
is a tiny fraction of a much
larger reality, and that as long
as we believe our perspective to be
unique is faulty. The veil helps us to
appreciate the fact that mortality is not
our natural dimension. We discover why we
are never entirely comfortable in our mortal
circumstances, and why we sometimes feel
like strangers and pilgrims on the earth.
Our experiences at the veil explain our
innate thrust always toward the future,
always beyond the horizon, and
always toward eternity.

The principles of the Gospel encourage us to be engaged and energized as we journey thru Babylon at an unhurried and yet a productive pace. It captivates us with its complexity. We are immersed in its intricacies, riveted by its rewards, and wrapped up in its wonders. It patiently anticipates our acknowledgement of its power to transform our lives and guide us to the gates of heaven. It waits upon our initiative.

The temple endowment blesses us with self-shaping, self-supporting, self-sustaining, and self-renewing characteristics. At its core, its doctrine becomes a perfectly liberating law that allows us to reach our potential in an atmosphere of mutually supportive inter-dependency with the Savior. His work and glory become our quest for the holy grail of immortality and eternal life in the Celestial Kingdom.

The endowment in
the temple releases our
energies to be creative, that we
might experience a greater capacity.
Its design is the perfect law of liberty.
The principles that relate to our welfare
have been thoroughly integrated into the
endowment. President Spencer W. Kimball
recognized its nurturing potential when he
urged us to lengthen our stride. Temple
worship blesses us with an awakening
sensitivity that puts us in touch
with our divine destiny.

The gentle
nudging of the Holy
Ghost provides us with the
regularly recurring reassurance of
a recalibration of our priorities that
auto corrects with a celestial precision.
He envelops us in an intuitive appreciation
of where we came from, why we are here, and
where we are going. He gives us the courage
to face the future with confidence and
to maintain our forward momentum
during the journey so we won't
lose our balance, fall down,
and possibly injure our
sensitive divine
nature.

It was from
before the foundation of the
world that celestial sparks were
struck off the divine anvil of God,
that were designed to ignite our desire
to repent and to be baptized. The scope
of His Plan is such that it encompasses
both immortal love and eternal life.
The eventual death of our body is
a horizon that is nothing, save
the limit of our sight, and
we perish only when we
have lost the vision
of our heavenly
home.

The Atonement of Jesus Christ is like a stethoscope that has the ability to detect our cardiac vital capacity. When our hearts have broken in contrition, the Savior recognizes their continuing sinus rhythm. It ratifies the congruence that exists between this life and the greater light of eternity when the miracle we call the Atonement has been galvanized in our behalf.

In our
stressful and
complex world, we
often see through a
glass darkly, making
it very difficult for us
to know how to harness
the energy of the elusive
equations found within
the powerful doctrine
that we are destined
thru foreordination
to live forever in
the kingdom
of God.

It is Christ's Atonement that generates repetitive opportunities to smell the delicious aroma of the bread of life that has been baking in a celestial oven. In anticipation of a buttered slice, we eagerly move along on the path that carries us closer to the threshold of our heavenly home.

Our
abiding faith
in the divine Plan
of our Father in Heaven
is confirmed in the temple,
where we learn that it has been
designed to bring us back into His
kingdom after we have grown up unto
the Lord, have spiritually matured,
and have demonstrated that the
basis of our hope of salvation
is in His Atonement, and
that alone.

The power
of Jesus Christ
is manifest in our
temple covenants, and
our solemn oaths trigger
a cleansing. The process of
our sanctification through the
Atonement allows us to draw near
to God's throne in heaven, from
which He will bestow upon our
heads the blessings we need,
instead of those that we
thought we had
wanted.

The Atonement
quickens the elements
of a Plan that, without it,
would stand in opposition to
eternal progression. With it,
mortality becomes the pathway
and portal to a joyful reunion
in the eternities, where we will
meet our loved ones before
the pleasing bar of God
at a homecoming that
is full of eternal
possibilities.

As
the fuel of
repentance fires
our determination
to follow the Savior,
His Atonement charges
our spiritual batteries as
it energize our vision with
an infinite perspective. With
an electrifying awareness, we
realize we can become holy
and without spot because
of the Lord's sacrifice
in our behalf.

Grace has the
power to raise us
up from physical death
by the resurrection, and
from spiritual death thru the
Atonement of Christ. We receive
the grace of God proportionately
as we conform to His standard of
personal righteousness that can
only be found in the teachings
of the Gospel of our Lord
and Savior Jesus Christ.

The endowment predisposes us to become all that God is, by incorporating His image and likeness into our own being and nature. For the endowment to fulfil its promises, we must care for the earthly tabernacles of our celestial spirits. It is only in the Atonement that we find a way for our corruptible bodies to become clean and pure, and full of light.

Since there
must be opposition
in all things, even as
there is faith, so must there
be its worldly counterparts. In
our day, the grip of fear paralyzes
many of God's children. Today, more
than ever, we need a hope in Christ. We
need the assurance of peace, that our
lives are moving in the direction of
our dreams. We are given enough
rope to hang ourselves, but the
Atonement can show us how
we can use it to lasso
the stars instead.

As we attend
the temple and
our testimony of
Christ swells in our
hearts, faith intensifies
our desire to repent. Our
effort to maintain temple
worthiness centers our lives,
to bring us into harmony with
true principles. As we endeavor
to be obedient, we find ourselves
in a constant state of improvement.
We begin to believe in ourselves,
and in God. Our hearts race
with the realization that our
progress might be headed
in the direction of
perfection.

We have
faith that
there is enough
room and enough
time in the eternities
for each of us develop
the capacity to see beyond
the limited horizon of our
vision all the way to the
Atonement of Christ, a
sacrifice that reaches
out to the best of us,
to the worst of us,
and to everyone
in between.

When we walk in the light of revealed truth, and we enter into life by way of the Atonement of Jesus Christ, we may be pleasantly surprised by the lavish accommodations that He has provided in the household of faith. His forgiveness removes the stains of sin from the linens, draperies, tapestries, and textiles upon which are embroidered all of the experiences that have embellished our lives.

The only certifiable fire retardant that can be dumped on the raging inferno of sin is the Atonement. Because of the Savior's sacrifice, we receive the kind of immortal body that we will need ensuing the resurrection, if we hope to dwell in another kind of fire, which is the divine fervor of eternal life.

It was Brigham Young's belief that "all organized existence is in progress either to an endless advancement in eternal perfections, or back to dissolution. There is no period in the eternities," he said, "wherein organized existence will become stationary, that it cannot advance in knowledge, wisdom, and power, and glory." Such is the mind expanding lesson of the law of eternal progression.

If we have
lived well, our
advancing years leave
us heavy with anticipation,
and we eagerly look forward to
the third act of the Three Act Play,
and to the final pages of the script,
where, having prayed ourselves hot,
we will read ourselves full and let
ourselves go, to live happily ever
after in the magical kingdom
where our dreams really will
come true and we will
enjoy true love's
kiss.

Repentance detoxifies us from the cares of the world and homogenization of our standards, even as we are subjected to the vicissitudes of life. It allows us to return to the hallowed halls of our faith, to be re-vitalized, as we are re-introduced to the star that shone above a lowly manger over two thousand years ago.

The line in all of our favorite fairy tales that reads: "...and they all lived happily ever after," is not written in the second act of life's Three Act Play, but in the third act. Nevertheless, in mortality, we get a foretaste of the happiness which has been prepared for the Saints, that awaits us just beyond the veil, each time we participate in the temple endowment.

In the House of the Lord, we slowly evolve into radiant beings. We witness an amazing truth: "That which is of God is light, and he that receiveth light, and continueth in God, receiveth more light, and that light groweth brighter and brighter until the perfect day." (D&C 50:24).

The
temple plots
our safe passage
thru the minefields
of mortality, documents
potential perils and pitfalls,
charts the recommended route
that leads to refuge, maps out
the success strategies we need
to follow if we wish to live
abundantly, and measures
our progress on the path
to perfection.

In the
form of photons,
sunrises and sunsets
are celestial lights and
the heavenly creations of
God. If we measure His light
in discrete energy packets, we
discover that time stands still for
both Him and photons. The photons
that were created at the moment of
the Big Bang, (remember that He said:
"Let there be light!") cannot be linked
to the age of the Universe because of
time dilation. For photons, as well as
for God, if both travel at the cosmic
speed limit, the Big Bang happened an
instant ago! But from our perspective,
however, although we view time as a
linear dimension, God has made it
possible for us to detect photons,
and thereby to conclude that He
must also exist, although it is
now 13.7 billion of our years
since His creation of the
evidence that would
support our
witness.

During the Millennium, the Savior "will reign personally upon the earth." (10th Article of Faith). This will permit members of the Church to enjoy unimpeded access to the temples, which will be as celestial family history centers where angelic mentors will assist them as they perform vicarious work for the dead at a rate that is unprecedented.

The family is where we go for triage, if we have been wounded by the adversary's fiery darts. It is a safe haven, where we confidently regroup, as we take hold of the horns of sanctuary. It is in the family that we learn about the order of heaven. It is there that the healing balm of Gilead may be massaged into our aching spiritual muscles, and where we may legally blood dope as we throw ourselves on the altar of sacrifice and the Atonement of Christ.

In an ordinance
that is a holy anointing,
temple patrons are blessed
with the power to come forth in
the morning of the first resurrection
as kings and priests, and queens and
priestesses, destined thru worthiness
to rule and reign in the House of
Israel forever. The ordinances
of the temple commemorate
and celebrate lives that
would have otherwise
remained forever
incomplete.

If it is true that "humanity has produced an astonishing 108 billion individual people over the past 50 millennia" (Source: Population Reference Bureau), how can we ever provide their vicarious temple work? To help to answer this question, Joseph Smith explained that "immortal beings will frequently visit the earth" during the millennium. "These resurrected beings will help with the government and other work." Thank God for His assistance, to help us accomplish a work that could never be done on our own.

The covenants
and the ordinances of the
temple reassure us that when the
task of securing our eternal legacy
has been completed, there will be no
gaps in our family history, there will be
no names missing from the book of life
that has been carefully compiled by the
angels in heaven, and there will be no
empty seats around the table, when
we all sit down together to enjoy
a reunion at family dinner in
our heavenly home.

The temple is
the place where we
go to shelter our spirits
and quiet our racing hearts.
We grasp the horns of sanctuary,
so that we might relieve the tensions
that always threaten to overwhelm us,
were we to allow ourselves to be caught
up and remain in the fast lane of life.
The temple is a time and place where
we can quietly reflect on the quality
of our preparation to live with our
Heavenly Father for all of
eternity.

The
temple reveals
that we have one foot
in heaven, and one foot in
time. The endowment makes
a determined effort to describe
God's perspective, but at the end
of the day, we remain trapped in
the present, and are able to only
indirectly appreciate eternity. We
come to the House of the Lord
over and over again, until
we finally get it right.
And then we do
it again.

The endowment in the temple is a shadow of that which is yet to come, and it cannot be understood at anywhere near the level of God's comprehension. As Paul wrote: "For now we see through a glass, darkly; but then face to face: now I know in part; but then shall I know even as also I am known." (1 Corinthians 13:12).

When we are
at one with God,
when we have spiritually
been born of Him and have
internalized His divine nature,
we will receive His image in our
countenances. That image and His
likeness will bridge the barriers of
time and space to leave an indelible
marker as a reminder of our noble
birthright. The temple endowment
rewrites the genetic code within
each of us, to bless our lives
with an unearthly quality
that is inherited from
our Heavenly Father.

"Spirits can only be revealed in flaming fire and glory." (Joseph Smith, "Times & Seasons," 4:331). Paul wrote that God can be best described as "a consuming fire" in the sense that His presence, His glory, is akin to fire, smoke and everlasting burnings. (Hebrews 12:29). When He reveals Himself, unveils the heavens, and His majesty fills the earth, the elements of our world will melt, the mountains will flow as rivers, valleys will be exalted, and rough places will be made smooth.

A number of
the chapters in the
story of our lives have
already been set to type,
and we aren't sure how many
remain to be written. But this we
know: The fairytale was created by
Heavenly Father, and we must honor
its premise that we are His daughters
and sons. We cannot start over and
make a new beginning, but we can
begin now, and with the guidance
of a very talented One Whose real
name is the Holy Ghost(writer),
we can pen a new ending to
the final chapters of the
tome that is entitled
The Plan of
God.

When The Plan endows us with faith in the power of Christ to save us from our sins, we will be profoundly motivated to live in accordance with His will. The Holy Ghost will bless each of us with eternal perspective. We will not only believe in Christ, but we will believe Christ, for the Spirit whispers to us that we have celestial potential. At the end of the day, The Plan teaches us that we are simply the work of God's hands.

We
enlarge the
foundations of
our spiritual center,
and we make room for
faith, even if the parts we
have been asked to play in
the drama of our lives seems
arduous. After we have signed
the papers, and we join other cast
members in the production of God's
Plan, we are reinvigorated to vividly
role-play, to animatedly pre-play, and
to repetitively re-play the lines we have
been asked to deliver in the theater of
life. Rehearsals that are conducted by
the Spirit will give us courage to be
worthy understudies to the Star of
the show, Who is revealed by the
storyboard of The Plan to be
none other than our Lord
and Savior, Jesus
Christ.

It is in
the temple,
that we are able
to see beyond our
mortal horizons. We
even have a name for
such a state, calling it
"the depths of eternity."
Our covenants bless us to
"inherit thrones, kingdoms,
principalities, powers, (and)
dominions, (of) all heights
and depths." (D&C 132:19).
The question remains: In
what direction will these
"heights and depths"
take us?

In a way, it is fortunate that the veil keeps us insulated from God's reality and grounds us on the solid and familiar bedrock of past, present, and future. For now, at least, the arrow of time moves in only one forward direction. This handy frame of reference permits us to live in an orderly fashion within a timeline woven in to the tapestry of the Gospel.

At the
veil, we
realize that
growing old is
strictly a quality
of mortality, and is
nothing more than a
brilliant mechanism that
has been designed by our
Heavenly Father that affords
us an opportunity to gauge the
approach of our reunion with
Him in the eternal world,
that will outlast time and
endure throughout
all eternity.

We attend the temple because God has already achieved His exaltation, while we, clearly, have yet to do so. The promises that we make with our Heavenly Father are as the passport visa stamps we need to be perfected. It is before the Recommend Desk that we move through Customs Control, to embrace the undiscovered country of His Kingdom.

As we
approach the
veil, we realize that
time is an artificial and
relative dimension in which
we can never be completely at
ease, for we are eternal beings.
We realize that time is transitory
by definition, and it is only our
perspective that makes it seem
that it is we who move thru
it, when it is really the
other way around.

The presence of the veil of the temple teaches us that a second order of mind exists. Our veil experiences repetitively reinforce the shadow of another world. We are reminded that the endowment, like so many other Gospel ordinances, cannot be exposed by the world. It is laced in symbolism, and it can only be spiritually discerned by those who have properly prepared themselves to receive the revelation of God.

We are
sanctified by our
temple worship. Our
"minds become single
to God, and the days will
come that (we) shall see him;
for he will unveil his face" unto
us. (D&C 88:68). We will no longer
be hobbled by limiting beliefs. "Now,
we see through a glass, darkly; but
then face to face; now (we) know
in part; but then shall (we) know
even as also (we are) known."
(1 Corinthinans 13:12).

As
nowhere
else, it is in
the temple that we
are cast off from the
limiting conditions and
self defeating behaviors that
would otherwise have blinded
us to a larger view of life. We
enjoy a settled conviction of
the truth. That peace follows
our obedience to celestial
principles that are taught
in the endowment and
that brings His Rest
within the reach
of our uplifted
hands.

If
we open
our hearts to
the Holy Ghost,
and allow ourselves
to be molded thru His
influence, we can be holy
and without spot. The Savior's
invitation to us to follow Him is
prefaced by the action verb "come."
As we undertake our journey to the
veil, we will be propelled beyond
an event horizon to a larger
view of life that is, for
the moment at least,
incomprehensible.

As we
come to the temple
with questions that have
been on our minds, we find
ourselves poised at the edge of
forever. We jump off into a stream
of revelation, to be carried along
in a quickening current that we
recognize is nothing less than
direct experience with God.
We dig deeply within our
faith to find the divine
guidance we will need
to take our bearings
on eternity.

The experiences of the temple that lead us to make good choices are essential to our eternal progression. How we respond to Heavenly Father's invitation to frequent His holy habitation will make a difference in regard to the blessings and opportunities that will be available to us down the road.

Our Heavenly
Father glories in
the possibility that we
might one day be like Him,
and offers us a special gift in
the temple; specifically His grace,
consisting of the endowment of
power by which we are brought
to His perfection and stature,
so that we may enjoy not
only what He has, but
also what He is.

Temple blessings are only important for those who, in the afterlife, are willing to accept the Gospel. Having said that, President Wilford Woodruff taught that almost all who live in the spirit world will accept vicarious ordinances when they are performed in their behalf. (See "Improvement Era," 11/1941).

About The Author

Phil Hudson and his wife Jan have 7 children and over 25 grandchildren. They enjoy spending time with their family at their cabin nestled in the Selkirk Mountains, on the shore of Priest Lake, the crown jewel of North Idaho. Phil had a successful dental practice in Spokane, Washington for 43 years, before retiring in 2015. He has an eclectic mix of hobbies, and enjoys the out of doors. He always finds time, however, to record his thoughts on his laptop, and understands Isaac Asimov's response when he was asked: "If you knew that you had only 10 minutes left to live, what would you do?" He answered: "I'd type faster."

Phil received the inspiration to write this book while he and Jan were serving as missionaries for The Church of Jesus Christ of Latter-day Saints, in the Kingdom of Tonga. While there, they celebrated their 50th wedding anniversary.

The Holy Ghost welcomes the trials we face, and views them as nothing more than pop quizzes in the learning laboratory of life. The Spirit sees the bigger picture and He is more invested in preparing us for the final exam that will come for each of us soon after our mortal curriculum has been concluded.

By The Author

Essays

    Spray from the Ocean of Thought
    Ripples on a Pond
    Serendipitous Meanderings
    Presents of Mind
    Mental Floss
    Fitness Training for the Mind and Spirit

First Principles and Ordinances Series

    Our Hearts are Changed
    A Broken Heart and a Contrite Spirit
    One Hundred and One Reasons Why We Are Baptized
    That We Might Have His Spirit To Be With Us
    This Do in Remembrance of Me

Book of Mormon Commentary

    Volume One: Born In The Wilderness
    Volume Two: Voices From The Dust
    Volume Three: Journey To Cumorah

Doctrine & Covenants Commentary

   Volume One - Sections 1 - 34
   Volume Two - Sections 35 - 57

Minute Musings: Spontaneous Combustions of Thought

   Volume One
   Volume Two
   Volume Three

Calendars:

   In His Own Words: Discovering William Tyndale
   As I Think About The Savior
   Scriptural Symbols

Children's Books

   Book of Mormon Hiking Song
   Happy Birthday
   Muddy, Muddy
   The Hiawatha Trail: An Allegory
   The Little Princess
   The Parable of The Pencil
   The Strange Tale of Huckelberry Henry
   The Thirteen Articles of Faith

Doctrinal Themes

- Are Christians Mormon? Volume One
- Are Christians Mormon? Volume Two
- Christmas is The Season When...
- Dentistry in The Scriptures
- Gratitude
- Hebrew Poetry
- Hiding in Plain Sight
- One Hundred Questions Answered by The Book of Mormon
- The House of The Lord
- Without The Book of Mormon
- Writing on Metal Plates
- The Highways and Byways of Life Volume One
- The Highways and Byways of Life Volume Two
- The Highways and Byways of Life Volume Three

A Thought For Each Day of the Year

- Faith
- Repentance
- Baptism
- The Holy Ghost
- The Sacrament
- The House of the Lord
- The Plan of Salvation
- The Atonement
- Revelation
- The Sabbath
- Life's Greatest Questions

Professional Publications

- Diode Laser Soft Tissue Surgery Volume One
- Diode Laser Soft Tissue Surgery Volume Two
- Diode Laser Soft Tissue Surgery Volume Three

If we are
so bold as to
internalize Gospel
principles, so that the
conduct of our lives is in
harmony with the law of the
Celestial Kingdom, we will be
free to partake of heavenly
gifts. Our path will lead to
the best machine for the
making of gods that
we know of: the
temple.

Quid magis possum dicere?

www.ingramcontent.com/pod-product-compliance
Lightning Source LLC
Chambersburg PA
CBHW060507240426
43661CB00007B/949